VISUAL QUICKSTART GUIDE

MICROSOFT EXPRESSION WEB 2

FOR WINDOWS

Nolan Hester

Peachpit Press

Visual QuickStart Guide
Microsoft Expression Web 2 for Windows
Nolan Hester

Peachpit Press
1249 Eighth Street
Berkeley, CA 94710
510/524-2178
510/524-2221

Find us on the Web at: www.peachpit.com

To report errors, please send a note to errata@peachpit.com

Peachpit Press is a division of Pearson Education

Editor: Clifford Colby
Production coordinator: David Van Ness
Composition: David Van Ness
Cover design: Peachpit Press
Indexer: Emily Glossbrenner

ISBN 13: 978-0-321-56379-8
ISBN 10: 0-321-56379-4

9 8 7 6 5 4 3 2 1

Printed and bound in the United States of America

To Mary

Special thanks to:

Clifford Colby and David Van Ness for their steady help in getting this second edition into your hands. Emily Glossbrenner for a thorough index that should prove a blessing to any reader stumped in the wee hours. As always, thanks to Nancy Aldrich-Ruenzel and Nancy Davis for making possible this life of working wherever my Web connection finds me.

Thanks also to the many participants in Microsoft's Expression Web discussion group who uniformly offered smart, patient answers. In the first edition, Wayne Smith, Tyler Simpson, and Anna Ullrich at Microsoft provided critical help and insights.

In the mid-stretch, Peet's Costa Rica Blend, Michael Franti and Spearhead's "Yell Fire!," and evening Frisbee sessions with Ceilidh kept me going.

TABLE OF CONTENTS

INTRODUCTION

Welcome to *Microsoft Expression Web 2 for Windows: Visual QuickStart Guide.* This program offers a powerful array of visual tools for creating great-looking sites while fully supporting Web-based standards. Standards may not be sexy but they're the driving force behind so many of the collaborative "Web 2.0" sites.

As a collaborative tool, Expression Web helps Web designers and coders work *together.* Expression Web makes it easy for designers to quickly design cool sites with tools that feel familiar. Thanks to Expression Web's underlying standards, you can pass those files over to coders, who can easily work on them in the development tools they prefer. When they're done, they can pass the work back to you and Expression Web without a hitch. Seamless back and forth—without your ever needing to touch the under-the-hood coding. (If you *want* to crawl into the XHTML, CSS, XML/XSLT, and schema, it's there. But the nice thing is that with Expression Web you don't *have* to.)

Standards but Cool Too

Does all this talk about standards sound too much like oat bran and vitamins? OK, let's cut to the chase: Expression Web comes with some of best style sheet tools on the market—and I say that as a long-time Dreamweaver user (**Figures i.1–i.2**) Can't figure out why one of your style changes doesn't seem to stick? Expression Web's CSS Properties tab shows you exactly where the cascade of formatting rules is thwarting your intentions. Ever tried to keep straight your internal and external styles? Expression Web makes it a click-and-drag affair (**Figure i.3**).

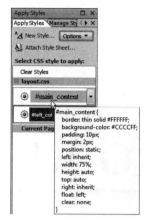

Figure i.1 What you see is what you get: Quickly find and apply a CSS style.

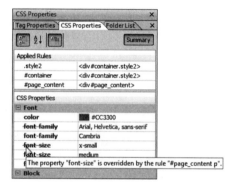

Figure i.2 The CSS Properties tab shows you exactly where the cascade of formatting rules is thwarting your styling intentions.

Figure i.3 Want to move internal styles to an external style sheet? Again, it's click and drag.

Still Using FrontPage?

If you're one of the many people who built their site using FrontPage, rest assured. Expression Web can open FrontPage sites without a hiccup. Because FrontPage uses so many nonstandard tools and bots, however, there are migration issues that you need to deal with. (For details, see "Bite the Bullet" on page 28.) FrontPage veterans also definitely need to take some time getting used to Expression Web's new digs. Don't expect to jump into Expression Web and build a new site on a hard deadline. Just remember: while Expression Web 2 is loaded with advanced options, none of those tools will keep you from using Expression Web's many beginner/intermediate features, So dive in even if, at first blush, it seems a bit intimidating.

So What's New in 2?

Virtually all the changes in Expression Web 2 are under the hood, so to speak. The main window, task panes, and tools remain virtually unchanged. But the beneath-the-surface changes are major and welcome. Expression Web 2 includes:

Figure i.4
The Insert menu offers quick access to ASP.NET server controls.

♦ New editing capabilities for Flash SWF and Windows Media files, a major hole in Expression Web's first version. (For more information, see page 181.)

♦ Support for Microsoft's new Silverlight-based plug-ins, which enable you to create rich, interactive pages. (For more information, see page 188.)

♦ Support for ASP.NET server controls (**Figure i.4**). Experienced coders will find a full range of controls within Expression Web 2 for creating Web applications and services (**Figure i.5**).

♦ Support for PHP pages and the server-based scripts used for database-driven Web sites (**Figure i.6**).

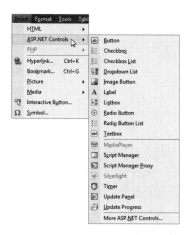

Figure i.5 The Toolbox offers even more ASP.NET controls, arranged by type.

With all these additions, Expression Web 2 now offers Web site tools for beginners to advanced coders. That's a wide range—too wide for this book, which remains focused on beginner/intermediate users. To learn about Microsoft's proprietary Silverlight and ASP.NET, start at silverlight.net and www.asp.net. If you want to learn more about using PHP with databases, take a look at Larry Ullman's terrific, *PHP and MySQL for Dynamic Web Sites: Visual QuickPro Guide* from Peachpit Press. Despite that Pro in the title, intermediate users will find Ullman's book very helpful: http://www.peachpit.com/store/product.aspx?isbn=0321526279.

Figure i.6 Expression Web 2 now offers built-in support for PHP pages.

Using This Book

Like all of Peachpit's Visual QuickStart Guides, this book uses lots of screenshots to guide you step by step through creating your Web pages and site. Succinct captions explain all of Expression Web's major functions and options. Ideally, you should be able to quickly locate what you need by scanning the page tabs, illustrations, and captions. Once you find a relevant topic, dig into the text for the details.

After showing you how to set up Expression Web to match your own way of working, the book gives you an overview of why you should focus on building a Web *site* rather than simply start making a single Web *page*. A big part of that approach involves using templates and CSS. I explain how you can use both to create a site that can smoothly grow larger over time—without drowning you in the scut work of constantly updating individual pages.

With that foundation under your belt, you can quickly start adding text and images to your pages and linking them together. Two chapters on CSS then walk you through how to style and position all that content to look terrific. By then, you'll be ready to dive into adding interactive behaviors and forms to give your site some polish. Finally, publishing it all couldn't be simpler. Really.

This book's companion Web site (www.waywest.net/expression) has example files from the book that you can download to work through the chapters step by step. Feel free to write me at books@waywest.net with your own tips—or any mistakes you may find. Good reading—and have a *great* Web site!

Tips

At the end of many tasks, you'll find tips on how to save time or use the many options tucked into Expression Web. Other features you'll find throughout the book include:

◆ **Code font:** When a word or words appear in code font, it's used to indicate the literal text you need to type in to Expression Web. For example: In the text window, type http://localhost and press Enter. Web addresses are also in code font.

◆ **Menu commands and keyboard shortcuts:** Menu-based commands are shown as: Choose File > Open Site. Keyboard-based shortcuts (when available) are shown in parentheses after the first step in which they can be used. For example: (Ctrl T) means that you can press the Ctrl and T keys at the same time to create a thumbnail version of an image.

EXPLORING EXPRESSION WEB

1

Whether you're running Windows XP or Windows Vista, you'll immediately recognize many of the interface features of Microsoft Expression Web 2. As with any program, however, you'll save yourself hours of later frustration by taking a quick look now to get an overall feel for Expression Web. So before you dive into creating Web pages and Web sites, let's explore its major windows, panes, and toolbars.

Opening and Closing Expression Web

For step-by-step information on creating new Web pages and sites, see Chapter 2 on page 17. For now, we'll just open Expression Web and take a look around.

To open Expression Web:

◆ Click the Start menu, and choose Microsoft Expression Web 2 from the pop-up list (**Figure 1.1**). When the program launches, a single blank page appears. You can then begin adding items to that page or open existing Web sites or pages.

To close Expression Web:

◆ Choose File > Exit. If you have not saved all your pages, Expression Web will ask if you want to save the changes. Click Yes to save them, and the program will then quit.

Figure 1.1 To open the program, click the Start menu and choose Microsoft Expression Web 2.

Using the Main Window

Expression Web's main window tidily displays most of the items you'll need day to day (**Figure 1.2**). In the center, the Editing window shows all your open documents, arranged in tabs. Task panes and toolbars flanking the Editing Window put your most commonly used tools a click away. You also can display or hide other panes and toolbars as you need them.

◆ **Web site files** (upper left, **Figure 1.2**): All of the current site's files and folders are displayed in the Folder List, one of four default task panes. The folder and page buttons in the pane's title bar make it simple to create new files right within the main site folder.

(continued)

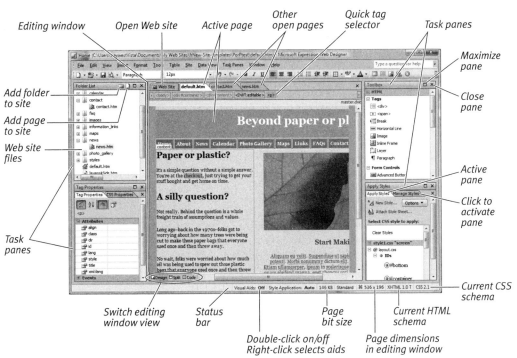

Editing window · Open Web site · Active page · Other open pages · Quick tag selector · Task panes

Maximize pane

Add folder to site

Add page to site

Web site files

Close pane

Active pane

Click to activate pane

Task panes

Current CSS schema

Switch editing window view · Status bar · Page bit size · Current HTML schema

Double-click on/off
Right-click selects aids

Page dimensions in editing window

Figure 1.2 Expression Web's main window includes most of the items you'll need day to day, with plenty of options for customization.

◆ **Editing window** (center, **Figure 1.2**): Tabs across the top denote open Web files and sites, enabling you to jump from file to file with a single click. As shown, the window is set to Design view, which hides all HTML and CSS coding. Code view shows only coding, while Split view lets you see both—an efficient compromise.

◆ **Task panes** (top right and bottom left, **Figure 1.2**): By default, two task panes run down the left of the Editing window and two down the right. For more information, see "Using the Task Panes" on page 7.

◆ **Status bar** (bottom, **Figure 1.2**): Running across the bottom of the window, the Status bar provides quick access to many HTML and CSS settings. **Visual Aids** help you work with usually hidden aspects of your pages. (For more information, see "Using the Visual Aids" on page 14.) Normally set to Auto with default schemas of XTML 1.0 Transitional and CSS 2.1 (the industry's current best-compromise choices), the **Style Application** can be changed with a double-click and choosing Manual from the toolbar that appears (**Figure 1.3**). Then you can double-click the **Standard** button to reach the Page Editor Options dialog box, where you can choose other schemas (**Figure 1.4**). Click the ▦ button if you need to change the standard width for your Web pages. (For more information, see "Setting Page Size" on page 6.) The last two items, the current HTML and CSS schemas, show the settings in the Page Editor Options dialog box.

Figure 1.3 The Style Application, normally set to Auto, can be switched to Manual using the toolbar's drop-down menu.

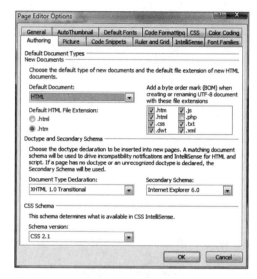

Figure 1.4 The Page Editor Options dialog box gives you complete control over Expression Web's default settings.

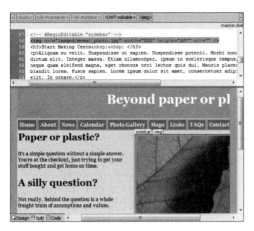

Figure 1.5 By default, Expression Web opens in the Split view, with the Code view above the Design view.

Figure 1.6 To switch your page view, choose View > Page and make a choice in the drop-down menu.

Figure 1.7 In the Editing window, click the tab of the page you want to see.

To switch Editing window views:

◆ By default, Expression Web opens in the Split view, with Code view at the top of the Editing window and Design view at the bottom (**Figure 1.5**). To switch out of this combination view, click the Design or Code buttons at the bottom-left of the Editing window (**Figure 1.2**).

or

◆ Use the keyboard shortcuts Ctrl Pg Up and Ctrl Pg Dn to cycle to the view you want.

or

◆ Choose View > Page, and make a choice in the drop-down menu (**Figure 1.6**).

✔ Tip

■ Whether you're a champion coder or designer who hates to see all that wiring, working in Split view helps you learn exactly how the code and design elements fit together.

To switch among open pages:

◆ At the top of the Editing window, click the tab of the page you want to see (**Figure 1.7**). Or cycle through the tabs using the keyboard shortcuts: Ctrl Tab and Ctrl Shift Tab.

USING THE MAIN WINDOW

Setting Page Size

Not so long ago, most Web designers built their layouts around a standard page width of about 750 pixels. As more and more home users have shifted to higher-resolution monitors, however, designers are shifting to a standard page of about 960 pixels. Whatever size you favor, Expression Web lets you easily set the dimensions of your Web pages.

To change the page size view:

◆ At the bottom-right of the status bar, click the ⊞ and choose another setting from the drop-down menu (**Figure 1.8**). Or choose View > Page Size and pick a setting in the drop-down menu (**Figure 1.9**). Release the cursor and the new size is applied immediately.

To modify a page size:

1. At the bottom-right of the status bar, click the ⊞ and select Modify Page Sizes in the drop-down menu (**Figure 1.10**). Or choose View > Page Size > Modify Page Sizes.

2. The Modify Page Sizes dialog box lists Expression Web's current page sizes. Choose the listing you want to change, and click Modify (top, **Figure 1.11**).

3. In the Page Size dialog box that appears, use the Width and Height input boxes to change the settings (bottom, **Figure 1.11**). Click OK to close the dialog box, and then Click OK to close the Modify Page Sizes dialog box as well. The new size replaces the previously listed size in the Status bar's drop-down menu (**Figure 1.12**).

✔ Tip

■ You can return to the original settings any time by clicking Reset in the Modify Page Sizes dialog box (top, **Figure 1.11**).

Figure 1.8 In the status bar, click the ⊞ and choose another setting from the drop-down menu.

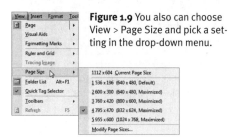

Figure 1.9 You also can choose View > Page Size and pick a setting in the drop-down menu.

Figure 1.10 To change the available choices, choose Modify Page Sizes in the drop-down menu.

Figure 1.11 In the Modify Page Sizes dialog box, choose a size in the list and click Modify (top). Use the Width and Height boxes to change the settings, and click OK to apply them (bottom).

Figure 1.12 The new size replaces the previously listed size in the drop-down menu.

SETTING PAGE SIZE

Figure 1.13 To open another pane, choose Task Panes and select it in the drop-down menu.

Figure 1.14 The selected pane appears, or a tab for it is added to an existing pane.

Using the Task Panes

By default, Expression Web displays four task panes: Folder List, Tag Properties, Apply Styles, and Toolbox. You can, however, display any of the 18 task panes, resize them as you please, and Expression Web will make that arrangement your default setup the next time the program opens.

Horizontal lines break the task panes drop-down menu into four groups (not including Reset Workspace Layout at the bottom (**Figure 1.13**). By default, items grouped together in the drop-down menu, such as Apply Styles and Manage Styles, will appear as separate tabs in the same pane. However, you can drag any tab into a pane of its own. (See "To rearrange task panes" on page 9.)

To open a task pane:

◆ From the Menu bar, choose Task Panes and the drop-down menu highlights the panes already open. To open another pane, select it in the drop-down menu (**Figure 1.13**). The selected pane appears, or a tab for it is added to an existing pane (**Figure 1.14**).

To close a task pane:

◆ Click the X button in the top-right corner of any tab or pane. The pane closes immediately.

✔ Tip

■ The Folder List pane can be toggled separately from the other panes by choosing View > Folder List or by pressing Alt F1 .

To switch tabs within a pane:

◆ Click any visible tab to make it active in the task pane, as indicated by the pane's title bar changing (**Figure 1.15**).

or

◆ If there are too many tabs within a task pane to see the one you need, click either arrow just below the title bar to scroll left or right to reach the desired tab (**Figure 1.16**). Then you can click that tab to make it active.

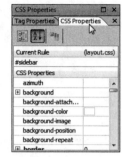

Figure 1.15 Click any tab to make it active in the task pane, as indicated by the title bar changing.

Figure 1.16 If the task pane has too many tabs to see at once, use the arrows to scroll left or right.

Figure 1.17 To create a free-standing task pane, click in the pane's title bar and drag it anywhere on your screen.

Figure 1.18 To redock a freestanding task pane, click in its title bar and, without releasing your cursor, drag it to either side of the Editing Window.

Figure 1.19 As a free-standing pane moves toward a docked pane, it snaps into the docked position.

Figure 1.20 Right-click in the title bar of a docked task pane, choose Float from the drop-down menu, and...

Figure 1.21 ...the task pane pops out of its docked position, surrounded by a dark border.

To rearrange task panes:

◆ Click in the title bar of any task pane and, without releasing your cursor, drag it anywhere on your screen to create a free-standing task pane (**Figure 1.17**).

or

◆ Click in the title bar of any free-standing task pane and, without releasing your cursor, drag it to either side of the Editing Window (**Figure 1.18**). As the free-standing pane moves close to the nearest docked pane, it snaps into the docked pane (**Figure 1.19**).

or

◆ Right-click in the title bar of a docked task pane, and choose Float from the drop-down menu (**Figure 1.20**). The task pane pops out of its docked position, surrounded by a dark border (**Figure 1.21**). You then can reposition and resize the pane to suit your needs (**Figure 1.22**).

Figure 1.22 You then can reposition and resize the pane as needed.

To restore the default pane positions:

◆ Choose Task Panes, and in the drop-down menu select Reset Workspace Layout (**Figure 1.23**). Expression Web closes all but the four default task panes and places them back on each side of the Editing window.

Figure 1.23 To restore the default pane positions, choose Task Panes and select Reset Workspace Layout.

To expand or collapse docked task panes:

◆ Click the small box button in the title bar of any pane with a long list of items, and the pane will expand to show more items (left, **Figure 1.24**). Click the button again to collapse a pane to its original compact form (right, **Figure 1.24**).

or

◆ Right-click in the title bar of the pane, choose Maximize from the drop-down menu, and the pane expands to show more items (left, **Figure 1.25**). Right-click in the title bar again, choose Restore from the drop-down menu, and the pane collapses to its original compact form (right, **Figure 1.25**).

Figure 1.24 Click the small box button in the title bar to expand a pane (left). Click the button again to collapse a pane (right).

Figure 1.25 Right-click in the title bar and choose Maximize to expand a pane (left). Right-click in the title bar again and choose Restore to collapse a pane (right).

USING THE TASK PANES

Figure 1.26 To see more of the Toolbox pane without expanding it, right-click in the title bar and choose Icons Only (left). The icons take up less space, so you can see more at a glance (right).

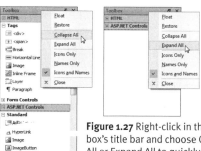

Figure 1.27 Right-click in the tool-box's title bar and choose Collapse All or Expand All to quickly compress or expand *all* the Toolbox pane's category listings.

Figure 1.28 To collapse a *single* category, click the ⊟ left of the bold-faced category name (left). To reveal a *single* category's listings, click the ⊞ (right).

✔ Tips

■ Expression Web's Toolbox pane, which contains more items than any other task pane, offers a way to see more of its contents without simply expanding it. Instead, right-click in the pane's title bar and choose Icons Only from the drop-down menu (left, **Figure 1.26**). The icons require less display space than icons with names, so you can see more at a glance (right, **Figure 1.26**). When you first start using Expression Web, you may need the names to know what the icons represent. But it doesn't take long to learn them, at which point you can switch to the more compact Icons Only view.

◆ You can fine-tune your view of the sprawling Toolbox pane as needed. Right-click in the title bar and choose Collapse All or Expand All to quickly compress or expand *all* the Toolbox pane's category listings (**Figure 1.27**). To collapse a *single* category, click the ⊟ left of the boldfaced category name (left, **Figure 1.28**). The listings disappear, leaving on the category name (right, **Figure 1.28**). To reveal a *single* category's listings, click the ⊞.

Using the Toolbars

Expression Web's 11 toolbars offer quick access to virtually every command you'll ever need. But having all of them visible at once would be a mess, so only the Common toolbar appears by default and offers, as the name suggests, the most commonly used commands. Much like the task panes, the toolbars can be repositioned and resized to suit your needs. Individual toolbars are explained throughout the book as the need for them arises.

To add a toolbar:

◆ From the Menu bar, choose View > Toolbars and choose a toolbar from the drop-down menu (**Figure 1.29**). The selected toolbar appears docked above the Editing window. (Toolbars already open appear with a check on the left side of the drop-down menu.)

✔ Tip

■ You also can open any toolbar by right-clicking in the title bar of an already open toolbar and making a choice in the drop-down menu that appears.

To close a toolbar:

◆ Click the X button in the top-right corner of any toolbar. The toolbar closes immediately.

or

◆ From the Menu bar, choose View > Toolbars and choose a toolbar that's already checked in the drop-down menu (**Figure 1.30**). Release your cursor and the selected toolbar closes immediately.

Figure 1.29 To add a toolbar, choose View > Toolbars and pick a toolbar in the drop-down menu.

Figure 1.30 To close a toolbar, choose View > Toolbars and pick a toolbar already checked in the drop-down menu.

Figure 1.31 To move a toolbar, move your cursor to the left end of the toolbar until it becomes a four-headed arrow (top). Then click and drag the toolbar to its new position (bottom).

Figure 1.32 To resize a toolbar, move your cursor to any edge of a toolbar until the cursor becomes a two-headed arrow (top). Click and drag the arrow and then release the cursor to enlarge or shrink that boundary of the toolbar (bottom).

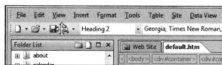

Figure 1.33 To redock a toolbar, click in the title bar and drag the toolbar toward the others docked above the Editing window (top). As the freestanding toolbar approaches the already docked toolbars, it snaps into position (bottom).

To move a toolbar:

◆ Move your cursor to the left end of the toolbar until it becomes a four-headed arrow (top, **Figure 1.31**). Click and drag the toolbar to its new position (bottom, **Figure 1.31**), which can be a freestanding box, a spot down the left-side of the main window, or above or below its present spot among the toolbars above the Editing window. Release the cursor and the toolbar stays in its new position.

To resize a toolbar:

◆ Move your cursor to any edge of a toolbar until the cursor becomes a two-headed arrow (top, **Figure 1.32**). Click and drag the arrow and then release the cursor to enlarge or shrink that boundary of the toolbar (bottom, **Figure 1.32**).

To redock a toolbar:

◆ Click in the toolbar's title bar or any blank area within the toolbar. When the cursor becomes a four-headed arrow, drag the toolbar toward the other toolbars docked above the Editing window (top, **Figure 1.33**). As the freestanding toolbar approaches the already docked toolbars, it snaps into position (bottom, **Figure 1.33**).

Using the Visual Aids

When you're working in Design or Split view, Expression Web offers you the option of displaying normally invisible elements. For example, it's much easier to adjust your layout when you can see the padding or margin for a particular element. You can select exactly which aids you want turned on and then show or hide them all at once.

To show or hide the visual aids:

◆ From the Menu bar, choose View > Visual Aids > Show (**Figure 1.34**). Repeat to hide the aids.

or

◆ Use press Ctrl + / to show or hide the aids.

or

◆ In the Status bar, double-click Visual Aids to switch from show to hide, or vice versa.

To turn on or off each visual aid:

◆ Once you activate the Visual Aids feature, choose View > Visual Aids and click each item you want made visible. You can turn on (or off) multiple items with a click, as long as your cursor remains in the drop-down menu (**Figure 1.35**). Move your cursor out of the drop-down menu area, and the aids you selected will turn on or off.

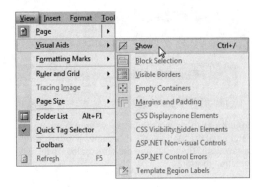

Figure 1.34 To show the visual aids, choose View > Visual Aids > Show. Repeat to hide the aids.

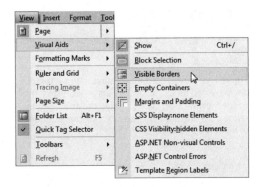

Figure 1.35 To turn on or off each visual aid, choose View > Visual Aids and click on each item you want made visible.

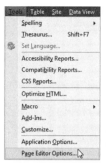

Figure 1.36 To change the Code view formatting, colors or text styling, choose Tools > Page Editor Options.

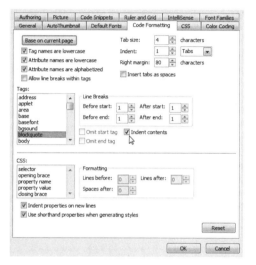

Figure 1.37 In the Code Formatting tab, set the line breaks and spacing you want surrounding a particular tag or CSS item.

Customizing Code and Design Views

Expression Web makes it easy to tweak how items are displayed in the Code or Design views. This can be especially helpful for coders, who often need to have their view set just so to help them find particular tags or code items. For example, you can set the number of line breaks or the margins for tabs surrounding specific attributes. Another option is assigning specific colors or text styling (such as bold or italic) to particular items. In version 2, HTML attributes now are displayed in alphabetical order, though you can change that if you like.

To change Code view formatting:

1. From the Menu bar, choose Tools > Page Editor Options (**Figure 1.36**).

2. Select the Code Formatting tab, where the first three check boxes are selected by default (**Figure 1.37**). Change the check box settings and tab settings as desired.

3. To change how a particular tag is displayed, select it in the Tags list and make your choices using the Line Breaks settings.

4. To change how a particular CSS item is displayed, select it in the CSS list and make your choices using the Formatting settings.

5. Once you finish setting each tag or CSS item you need to change, click OK to close the dialog box and apply your choices.

✔ Tips

- If you already have a page set up as you like it, open it before beginning these steps. Then in step 3, click the Base on current page button.

- If you change your mind and want to restore Expression Web's original settings, click Reset in step 3.

To change Code view colors or styling:

1. From the Menu bar, choose Tools > Page Editor Options (**Figure 1.36**).

2. Select the Color Coding tab, where the Code view settings button is active by default (**Figure 1.38**).

3. To change how a particular item is displayed, select it in the left-side list and use the right-side drop-down menus and checkboxes to set how an item is colored or its text styled.

4. Repeat step 3 for any other items in the Display items list that you want. Click OK to close the dialog box and apply your choices.

✔ Tip

■ To restore Expression Web's original settings, click Reset Defaults in step 3.

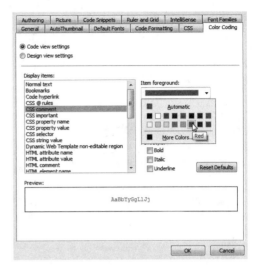

Figure 1.38 In the Color Coding tab, set the coloring and text styling you want applied to a particular display item.

2

CREATING SITES

No doubt you're eager to begin creating Web pages, but hold up. More than likely, your real goal is to create a Web *site* of pages that share a similar look and a common navigation system. And that's a lot harder to do using a one-page-at-a-time approach. So this chapter starts by showing how to create a blank, one-page site. Then the rest of the chapter focuses on how to create a unified, multiple-page site using Expression Web's templates, which are based on Cascading Style Sheets (CSS). That approach offers two bonuses: your pages display faster and more reliably, plus it's way easier to update them as your site grows. For more information on creating individual Web pages, see Chapter 3 on page 35.

To create a new blank Web site:

1. Choose File > New > Web Site (**Figure 2.1**).

2. In the New dialog box that appears, General is automatically selected so in the middle pane choose One Page Web Site (or Empty Web Site) (**Figure 2.2**).

3. By default, Expression Web offers to save the site at ...\UserName\Documents\ and name it *My Web Sites* (in Windows Vista) or *mysite* (Windows XP). Instead, consider clicking Browse and navigating to a place *outside* the Documents folder, perhaps on a separate hard drive (see "Where to Save Local Sites?" on page 19). Once you select or create a new folder in the New Web Site Location dialog box, click Open (**Figure 2.3**).

Figure 2.1 To create a new blank Web site, choose File > New > Web Site.

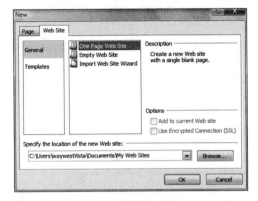

Figure 2.2 In the New dialog box that appears, select General and choose One Page Web Site or Empty Web Site.

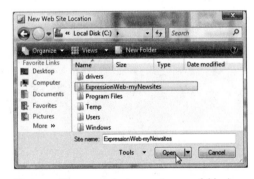

Figure 2.3 Once you select or create a new folder in the New Web Site Location dialog box, click Open.

Figure 2.4 When the New dialog box reappears, the site's path and folder are listed in the text box (top). Add the name for the new site after the backward slash, and click OK (bottom).

Figure 2.5 A dialog box appears briefly while the site is generated.

Figure 2.6 The Web Site tab at the top of the Editing Window lists the site's files—in this case a single, blank home page, default.htm.

4. When the New dialog box reappears, the path and folder are listed in the bottom text box (top, **Figure 2.4**). Type the name you want to use for the new site after the backward slash, and click OK (bottom, **Figure 2.4**).

5. A dialog box appears briefly while the site is generated (**Figure 2.5**). A Web Site tab then appears at the top of the Editing Window, listing the site's files— in this case a single, blank home page, default.htm (**Figure 2.6**). The same list also appears in the Folder List task pane to the left. You now can add content to the blank page or create more pages for the site.

✔ Tip

■ To help you build a full-styled Web site more quickly, Expression Web includes a variety of CSS-based templates and style sheets. For more information, see "Creating Template-based Sites" on the next page.

Where to Save Local Sites?

Even though Expression Web offers to save the local versions of your Web sites within your profile directory (...\UserName\Documents\), that doesn't mean it's a good idea. Many Web pros prefer to save their sites on a separate drive or, at least, outside the UserName folder. That way if the UserName directory, your most-used directory, gets corrupted, your Web files remain safe.

CREATING A BLANK WEB SITE

Creating Template-based Sites

Using an Expression Web site template to start your own Web site can save so much time that it's worth learning all the required steps—picking a template, customizing the template's content, and then replacing the site's other pages with your own content. By using a template, you can change sitewide items, such as the masthead and navigation links, in one place and have them automatically updated on all your pages. Best of all, behind the scenes Expression Web automatically generates the necessary CSS files for your site, ensuring uniform display in as many Web browsers as possible (**Figure 2.7**).

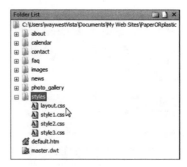

Figure 2.7 The bonus of creating template-based sites: Behind the scenes, Expression Web automatically generates all the necessary CSS files.

To select and customize Web site templates:

1. Choose File > New > Web Site.

2. In the New dialog box that appears, select Templates in the left column and use the middle list and right-hand Preview area to find the template that best suits your needs (**Figure 2.8**).

3. Click OK to select the site template. A dialog box appears briefly while the site is generated. A tab for the new template-based site appears at the top of the Editing Window, with all the site's files listed in the window and adjacent Folder List (**Figure 2.9**).

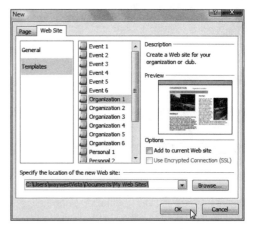

Figure 2.8 Select Templates in the left column and then use the middle list and right-hand Preview area to find the template that suits your needs.

Figure 2.9 The Editing Window's site tab, along with the adjacent Folder List, list all the files generated by the template.

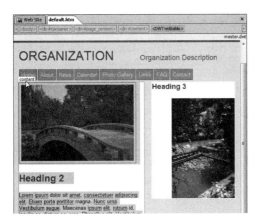

Figure 2.10 Selectable areas in the template-based page can be replaced with your own headlines, text, or images.

Figure 2.11 Other areas of the template-based page cannot be clicked or changed directly because they are shared by multiple pages.

Figure 2.12 To open locked template areas, double-click the .dwt file (usually master.dwt) in the Folder List.

4. Double-click default.htm to open the site's home page. When the page opens, some areas can be clicked, which means their contents can be replaced with your own headlines, text, or images (**Figure 2.10**). Other areas of the page, such as the site's name and navigation bar, cannot be clicked or changed directly because they are shared by multiple pages (**Figure 2.11**).

5. To open these locked, sitewide areas, double click the .dwt file (usually named master.dwt) in the Folder List (**Figure 2.12**).

(continued)

CREATING TEMPLATE-BASED SITES

6. When the template page opens, its contents can be clicked and changed (**Figure 2.13**). Select and replace the elements used by multiple pages, such as the site name and navigation labels, as needed (**Figure 2.14**).

7. Right-click the tab of the .dwt (master) page, and choose Save from the drop-down menu (**Figure 2.15**). A status dialog box warns that several files will be updated by saving your changes to the master template page (top, **Figure 2.16**). Since that's exactly what you want to do, click Yes and then click OK to close the status dialog box (bottom, **Figure 2.16**).

8. Switch back to your home page by clicking its tab, and the changes in the template page have been applied (**Figure 2.17**). The * in the page's tab, however, means the changes have not been saved, so choose File > Save All. You now can replace heads, text, and images on the home page to suit your needs, as explained in the next section "Replacing Content in Template-based Sites."

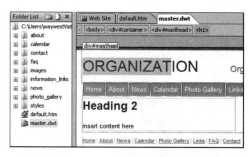

Figure 2.13 Once open, all the template page's contents can be selected and replaced with your own headings, text, and images.

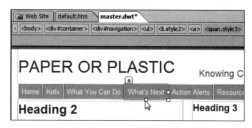

Figure 2.14 Changes in the template page to sitewide items, such as the masthead and navigation labels, are applied to all your pages.

Figure 2.15 Right-click the tab of the .dwt (master) page, and choose Save from the drop-down menu.

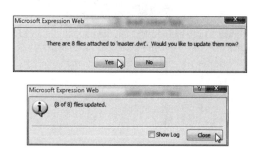

Figure 2.16 Click Yes when a dialog box warns that the template changes will update multiple pages (top). Once Expression Web updates the pages, click Close (bottom).

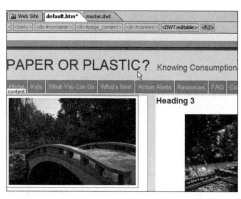

Figure 2.17 Back in your home page, the template changes appear in the updated masthead and navigation labels.

Figure 2.18 To replace template-based content with your own, select a heading.

Figure 2.19 Type or paste in a heading of your own, and the styling of the template's original heading is applied automatically.

Figure 2.20 To replace text in template-based page, just select it...

Figure 2.21 ...and type or paste in your own text, which is automatically styled to match the template's original text.

Replacing Content in Template-based Sites

Once you customize the sitewide master template (see page 20), you can very quickly replace the content in any pages with your own heads, text, and images. The image inserted in step 6 was sized ahead of time for the space. For more information on inserting and sizing images, see Chapter 5 on page 79.

To replace template content with your own:

1. Double-click or click and drag to select a heading in your template-based page (**Figure 2.18**).

2. Type or paste in a heading of your own. The styling of the template's original heading is applied automatically to your own heading (**Figure 2.19**).

3. Select a paragraph of text in your template page (**Figure 2.20**).

4. Type or paste in your own text. The styling of the template's original text is applied (**Figure 2.21**).

5. Click an image in the template to select it (**Figure 2.22**).

(continued)

Figure 2.22 Click an image to select it in the template-based page.

REPLACING CONTENT IN TEMPLATE-BASED SITES

6. Choose Insert > Picture, and make a source choice from the drop-down menu (**Figure 2.23**).

7. Navigate to the image you want to use, and click Insert (**Figure 2.24**).

8. Add a brief description to the Alternate text field, and click OK (**Figure 2.25**). Your image replaces the original image in the template-based page (**Figure 2.26**). Be sure to save your changes ([Ctrl][S]).

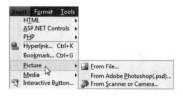

Figure 2.23 Choose Insert > Picture, and pick a source in the drop-down menu.

Figure 2.24 Navigate to the image you want to use, and click Insert.

Figure 2.25 Add a brief description to the Alternate text field (and a long description if you like), and then click OK.

Figure 2.26 Your image replaces the original image in the template-based page.

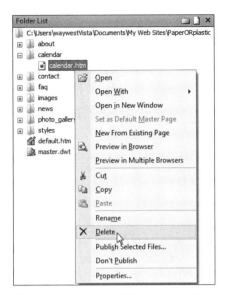

Figure 2.27 In the site's Folder List pane, right-click the page you don't need and choose Delete.

Figure 2.28 Double-check that you've chosen the right file, and click Yes.

Figure 2.29 The selected file disappears from the Folder List while its enclosing folder remains.

Deleting or Adding Pages to Template Sites

Naturally the site you create using Expression Web's templates won't use the exact number pages found in the prebuilt site. Getting rid of unnecessary pages is simple enough. But a few extra steps are required to ensure that any pages you add to the site are still based on those templates you've so carefully updated with your own content.

To delete pages from your template-based site:

1. In the site's Folder List pane, right-click the page you don't need and choose Delete from the drop-down menu (**Figure 2.27**).

2. When the Confirm Delete dialog box appears, double-check that you've chosen the right file and click Yes (**Figure 2.28**). The selected file disappears from the Folder List while its enclosing folder remains (**Figure 2.29**).

✔ Tip

■ To delete an entire folder of unneeded pages and the folder holding them, right-click the *folder* within the Folder List pane and choose Delete from the drop-down menu.

DELETING PAGES FROM TEMPLATE SITES

To add template-based pages to your site:

1. In the site's Folder List pane, right-click the page whose basic elements you want to use in a new page and choose New From Existing Page from the drop-down menu (**Figure 2.30**).

   A new untitled page appears in the Editing Window containing the same content and formats as the template-based page (**Figure 2.31**).

2. Choose File > Save, and the Save As dialog box appears, automatically opening to show your site (**Figure 2.32**).

3. Navigate to the site subfolder where you want to save the new page—typically the same folder where the existing page resides.

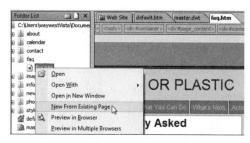

Figure 2.30 To add template-based pages to your site, right-click a page in the Folder List and choose New From Existing Page.

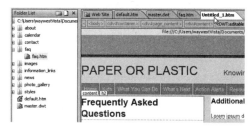

Figure 2.31 A new untitled page appears containing the same content and formats as the template-based page.

Figure 2.32 Navigate to the site subfolder where you want to save the new page.

Figure 2.33 Give the new page a distinctive name, and click Save.

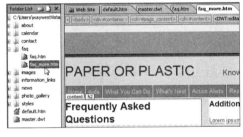

Figure 2.34 The new page appears within the chosen folder in the Folder List pane.

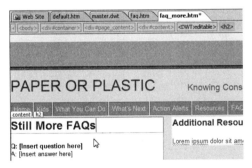

Figure 2.35 Now you can add content to the new page while maintaining the formatting and design of the previous page.

4. Type a distinctive name in the File name text box, and click Save (**Figure 2.33**).

The new page appears within the chosen folder in the Folder List pane (**Figure 2.34**).

5. Now you can add content to the new page while maintaining the formatting and design of the previous page (**Figure 2.35**). Remember, if the Editing Window tab displaying a file's name includes *, you need to save your changes.

✔ Tip

■ Before creating a new page from an existing one, add any content to the first page that you'll also want to appear on the new pages, such as shared headings.

Importing a Web Site

If you've already built a Web site using another program, Expression Web does not force you to start from scratch. Instead you can import the entire site, either from your hard drive or where it's posted on the Web. For anyone who created a site using FrontPage, Microsoft's previous Web-creation program, this can be a life-saver. (FrontPage site builders migrating to Expression Web should read the *Bite the Bullet* sidebar on this page.)

Bite the Bullet

There's good and bad news for anyone who has a Web site built with FrontPage, Microsoft's previous Web-creation program. The good news: Expression Web will recognize many of the proprietary FrontPage server extensions (FPSE) that drove much of its behind-the-curtain magic. Expression, for example, won't mess up the display of such extension-based items as Shared Borders or FrontPage Themes. But the bad news is that you won't be able to use Expression to add those things to *new* pages. As a result, your site over time may begin to look like two people in a horse suit heading in opposite directions.

The dilemma arises precisely because Expression Web uses current Web standards and, so, avoids the sort of proprietary coding found in FrontPage. That coding worked fine in Microsoft's own Internet Explorer browser, but many other browsers couldn't render it correctly.

To help FrontPage users recognize the new terrain, Expression Web uses some of the same terms. But the coding driving the new program is quite different. The transition may be painful, but the best long-term strategy probably boils down to abandoning those FrontPage bots and extensions. Bite the bullet now, and later on you'll be glad you did. For the latest details on making the switch, go to http://download.microsoft.com/download/f/f/2/ff2d736a-9ec6-4e3b-b094-d782aa7cda72/Microsoft_FrontPage_to_Expression_Web.doc.

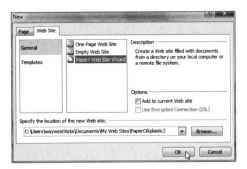

Figure 2.36 To import a Web site, choose the Import Web Site Wizard in the New dialog box.

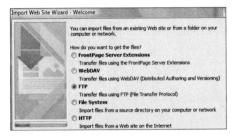

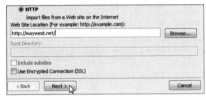

Figure 2.37 The Import Web Site Wizard asks which of five methods to use to import the Web site (top). After making your choice, either enter a path or Web address or click Browse to navigate to your destination and click Next (bottom).

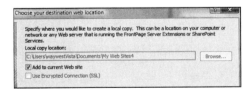

Figure 2.38 Browse to where the site should be imported, or if a site is already open in Expression Web, select Add to current Web site.

To import a Web site:

1. Choose File > New > Web Site.

2. In the New dialog box, choose General > Import Web Site Wizard and click OK. (**Figure 2.36**).

3. The Import Site Wizard starts by asking you which method to use to import the Web site (top, **Figure 2.37**). Click one of the five radio buttons and then either type the path or Web address or click Browse to navigate to your destination. Click Next to proceed (bottom, **Figure 2.37**).

4. Use the Browse button in the next dialog box to pick where to import the site, or if a site is already open in Expression Web, select Add to current Web site. (**Figure 2.38**). Then click Next.

(continued)

5. The next dialog box lets you control how many levels below the home page you want to import (**Figure 2.39**). Or you can limit the import to a maximum size or only HTML and image files. Click Next.

6. Click Finish in the final dialog box of the Import Site Wizard and a progress dialog box tracks the download (**Figure 2.40**).

7. Assuming you still want to replace the current site's home page with that of the imported site, click Yes (**Figure 2.41**).

The imported site's home page will open in Expression Web with the rest of the site's files visible in the Folder List pane (**Figure 2.42**). You now can update or expand the site using Expression Web.

Figure 2.39 Choose how many levels below the home page you want to import. Or limit the import to a maximum size or only HTML and image files.

Figure 2.40 Once the import begins, a progress dialog box tracks the download.

Figure 2.41 If you want to replace the current site's home page with that of the imported site, click Yes.

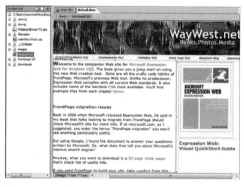

Figure 2.42 Expression Web displays the imported site's home page and lists the rest of the site's files in the Folder List.

Figure 2.43 To close a Web site after saving your changes, choose File > Close Site.

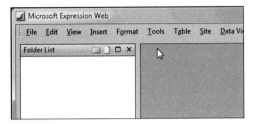

Figure 2.44 The Web site closes, leaving an empty Folder List and Editing Window.

Working with Web Sites

To avoid breaking any of the links within your Web sites, you should always use Expression Web to close, open, rename, or delete sites.

To close a Web site:

◆ After choosing File > Save All, choose File > Close Site (**Figure 2.43**).

The Web site closes, leaving an empty Folder List and Editing Window (**Figure 2.44**).

✔ Tip

■ You do not have to close one site to open another. See the second Tip for "To open a site" on the next page.

To open a Web site:

1. Choose File > Open Site (**Figure 2.45**).

The Open Site dialog box appears, listing all the Web sites you've created using Expression Web (**Figure 2.46**).

2. Select one in the right column, and click Open.

The selected site appears in the Editing Window, with its path displayed across the top of the window (**Figure 2.47**).

✔ Tips

■ In step 2, if you double-click a Web site in the list, Expression Web says "No items match your search." Always use the Open button.

■ You can have multiple sites open at the same time. After opening one site, repeat steps 1 and 2, only this time navigating to another Web site. Expression Web opens each successive site in a separate window (**Figure 2.48**).

■ To have Expression Web automatically display the last opened site when it starts up, choose Tools > Application Options. In the dialog box that appears, check Open last Web site automatically when Expression Web starts.

■ To see *only* your recently opened Web sites, in step 2, click the Web Sites button in the left column of the dialog box. Or choose File > Recent Sites and pick a listing in the drop-down menu.

Figure 2.45 To open a Web site, choose File > Open Site.

Figure 2.46 The Open Site dialog box lists all the sites you've created using Expression Web.

Figure 2.47 The site you select to open appears in the Editing Window, with its path displayed across the top of the window.

Figure 2.48 When opening multiple Web sites, Expression Web opens each one in a separate window.

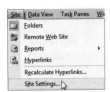

Figure 2.49 To rename an open Web site, choose Site > Site Settings.

Figure 2.50 In the Site Settings dialog box, the current name is highlighted (top). Type a new name and click OK to apply the change (bottom).

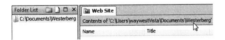

Figure 2.51 The site's name changes in the Editing Window's path as well as in the Folder List.

Figure 2.52 To delete a open Web site, right-click its name in the Folder List pane and choose Delete.

Figure 2.53 Make sure Delete this Web site entirely is selected and then click OK, and the site will be deleted immediately.

To rename a Web site:

1. Open the site you want to rename and choose Site > Site Settings (**Figure 2.49**).

   When the Site Settings dialog box opens, the current name is highlighted in the Web name text box (top, **Figure 2.50**).

2. Type a new name and click OK to close the dialog box and apply the change (bottom, **Figure 2.50**).

   The site's name changes in the path within the Editing Window as well as in the Folder List (**Figure 2.51**).

To delete a Web site:

1. Open the site you want to delete. Right-click its name in the Folder List pane, and choose Delete from the drop-down menu (**Figure 2.52**).

2. When the Confirm Delete dialog box appears, make sure Delete this Web site entirely is selected and click OK (**Figure 2.53**).

   The selected site no longer appears in the Folder List pane.

✔ Tip

- You cannot undo the deletion, so it might be wise to let no-longer-needed sites sit idle for a few days rather than deleting them immediately—and regretting it immediately as well.

Switching the Web Site View

By default, Expression Web displays an open Web site as a list of folders and files (**Figure 2.54**). However, depending on the task at hand, you can switch your view of the Web site to three other views. For more information on the Remote Web Site choice, see "Publishing the Site" on page 231.

To switch your Web site view:

◆ At the top of the Editing Window, click the site's tab. Then at the bottom of the Editing Window, click the Remote Web Site button to either set up the remote publishing site or see the files you've already uploaded (**Figure 2.55**).

or

◆ Click the site's tab in the Editing Window and then at the bottom click the Reports button for a status list and possible problems with the site (**Figure 2.56**).

or

◆ In the Folder List pane, select a file for which you want link information. At the top of the Editing Window, click the site's tab. Then at the bottom of the Editing Window, click the Hyperlinks button to see a diagram of all the inbound and outbound links for the selected file **Figure 2.57**).

Figure 2.54
By default, Expression Web displays an open Web site as a list of folders and files.

Figure 2.55 Click the Remote Web Site button to either set up a remote site for publishing or see the files already uploaded.

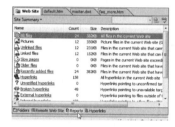

Figure 2.56
Click the Reports button for a site status list and possible problems.

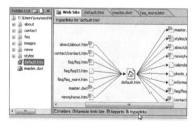

Figure 2.57 Click the Hyperlinks button to see a diagram of all the inbound and outbound links for a particular Web page.

WORKING
WITH PAGES

Having set up a Web site in Chapter 2, you're ready to create individual pages. This chapter also covers other page basics, such as saving, renaming, retitling, and deleting pages. Finally, you'll learn how to preview your pages in a variety of Web browsers.

Creating Web Pages

As in creating Web sites, you have two routes to go: start from scratch with a blank page or use a CSS-based template page. Depending on the situation, you'll probably do a little of both. If you've created a lot of pages before, starting with a blank page may be perfect for your needs. If you're looking to learn the ins and outs of CSS, however, starting with one of Expression Web's CSS-based page templates can save time by giving you a jump start. "To create a new CSS-based page" on page 38 offers a quick overview; it's covered in depth in "Creating Layouts with CSS" on page 147.

To create a new blank page:

1. Open the Web site in which you want to work, and choose File > New > Page (**Figure 3.1**).

   When the New dialog box appears, HTML is selected automatically (**Figure 3.2**). (To change that, see last tip on the next page.)

2. Click OK, and a new blank Web page appears in the Editing Window (**Figure 3.3**).

Figure 3.1 To create a new blank page, choose File > New > Page.

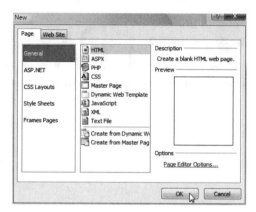

Figure 3.2 HTML is selected automatically in the New dialog box.

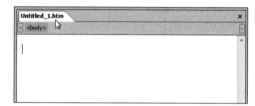

Figure 3.3 A new blank Web page appears in the Editing Window ready for your content.

Figure 3.4 You also can create a new page by clicking the New button in the Common toolbar.

Figure 3.5 A New button also resides in the Folder List's title bar.

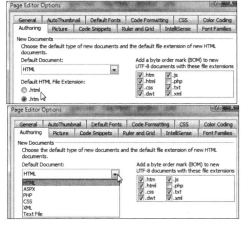

Figure 3.6 The Authoring tab in the Page Editor Options dialog box lets you change the default HTML *file extension* (top) or the *document type* used for new pages (bottom).

✔ Tips

■ In step 1, if you want to use a standard, HTML-based Web page, choose File > New > HTML and a blank Web page appears without going through the New dialog box. Or if the Common toolbar is visible, click the New button (**Figure 3.4**).

■ If you're adding pages to an existing site, you also can click the New button in the Folder List's title bar, which by default also creates a new HTML page (**Figure 3.5**).

■ While you could create a free-standing page without first opening a Web site, you'll avoid potential file chaos by working within an already created site—even if it's a site with just a single page.

■ In step 1, if you want to use a format other than HTML for a *single page*, click another choice—such as CSS— in the middle column (**Figure 3.2**).

■ To change the default format for *all new pages*, choose Tools > Page Editor Options and click the Authoring tab in the Page Editor Options dialog box (**Figure 3.6**). Expression Web 2 lets you switch the HTLM file extension from .html (now the default) to .htm (top, **Figure 3.6**). Or use the Default Document drop-down menu to choose an entirely different format, such as PHP or CSS (bottom, **Figure 3.6**). Click OK to close the dialog box and apply the change.

To create a new CSS-based page:

1. Open the Web site in which you want to work, and choose File > New > Page.

2. When the New dialog box appears, select CSS Layouts in the left column and make a choice in the middle column based on the Preview area (**Figure 3.7**).

3. Click OK, and an untitled—and apparently blank—page appears in the Editing Window (**Figure 3.8**).

4. To really see what's going on, turn on Expression Web's visual aids. Choose View > Visual Aids > Show ([Ctrl][+]) (**Figure 3.9**), and then select all but the two ASP.NET items in the drop-down menu (**Figure 3.10**).

   The previously blank page now shows a rough version of the step 2 preview (**Figure 3.11**).

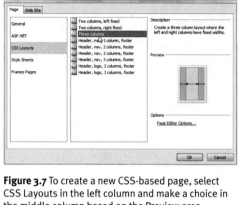

Figure 3.7 To create a new CSS-based page, select CSS Layouts in the left column and make a choice in the middle column based on the Preview area.

Figure 3.8 Underwhelming: a blank CSS-based page with all the visual aids turned off.

Figure 3.9 To see what's going on in a CSS-based page, choose View > Visual Aids > Show.

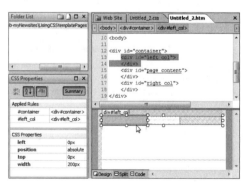

Figure 3.11 The previously blank page now shows a rough version of the step 2 preview. For an even better sense of how the page works, switch to Split View and turn on the CSS Properties task pane.

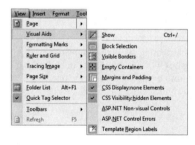

Figure 3.10 In the Visual Aids drop-down menu, select all but the two ASP.NET items.

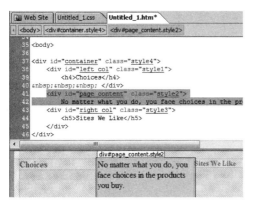

Figure 3.12 Once you can see the page's CSS-based layout sections in the Design and Code windows, you can start adding content.

Figure 3.13 Expression Web automatically generates a companion CSS file for the page you create.

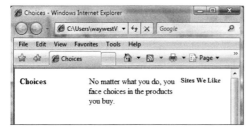

Figure 3.14 To see how the still rough CSS-based page looks, take a quick peek using your Web browser.

5. Now that you can see the page's CSS-based layout sections—known as divs—in the Design and Code windows, you can start adding content (**Figure 3.12**).

6. Be sure to save your changes. When you do, Expression Web will ask you to name and title the HTML page and its related CSS file (**Figure 3.13**).

7. Though the page remains far from done, press F12 to see how it looks at the moment in your default Web browser (**Figure 3.14**).

✔ Tips

■ In step 4, for a better sense of how the page works, switch to Split View and turn on the CSS Properties task pane.

■ For lots more detail on laying out pages using CSS, including sources for other CSS templates, see "Creating Layouts with CSS" on page 147.

Working with Web Pages

To avoid breaking any of the links among your Web pages, use Expression Web (rather than the Windows Explorer) to save, open, change the name or title, or delete pages.

To save a Web page:

1. Choose File > Save ($\boxed{\text{Ctrl}}\boxed{\text{S}}$) or click the Save button in the Common toolbar or right-click the page's tab and choose Save from the drop-down menu (**Figure 3.15**).

2. If this is the first page you've saved to the site, the Save As dialog box automatically names the file default, making it the site's home page (**Figure 3.16**). (See second tip on the next page.) The dialog box also automatically titles the page Untitled1. If that's your intention, click Save and the file is saved with that name and title and the dialog box closes.

   or

   To give the file another name and title, type the name in the File name text box and click Change title (**Figure 3.17**). When the Set Page Title appears, replace the automatic title (top, **Figure 3.18**) with the one you want to use (bottom, **Figure 3.18**). Click OK to close the dialog box.

Figure 3.15 You have at least three ways to save a page.

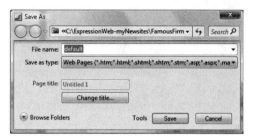

Figure 3.16 If this is the first page you've saved to the site, the Save As dialog box automatically names it default, making it the site's home page.

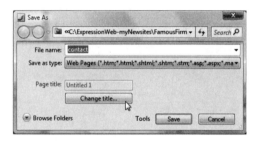

Figure 3.17 Use the File name field to rename the page, and then click Change title.

Figure 3.18 Type a new title (top), and click OK to close the dialog box (bottom).

Figure 3.19 The Save As dialog box reappears with your name and title choices in place. Click Save to apply the changes and close the dialog box.

Figure 3.20 The new name appears in the Folder List and the open page tab.

Figure 3.21 A page's file name (top) is not its title, which appears in the browser's title bar and page tab (bottom).

Figure 3.22 To designate another file as the home page, right-click it in the Folder List and choose Set as Home Page.

3. The Save As dialog box reappears with your name and title choices in place (**Figure 3.19**). Click Save to apply the changes and close the dialog box.

The new name appears in the Folder List and the open page tab (**Figure 3.20**).

✔ Tips

- A page's *name* is the file name in your directory (for example, `default.htm`), while the *title* is what your Web visitors see in their browser's title bar when they open the page (**Figure 3.21**).

- You can designate another file as a site's home page at any time. Right-click the file in the Folder List, and choose Set as Home Page in the drop-down menu (**Figure 3.22**). Click Yes when the confirmation dialog box appears, and the selected page is renamed `default.htm` and the previous home page is named `default-old.htm` (**Figure 3.23**).

Figure 3.23 Click Yes when the confirmation dialog box appears (top). The selected page is renamed `default.htm` and the previous home page named `default-old.htm`.

To open a Web page:

Do one of the following:

◆ To open a Web page in the *same* Web site, double-click its name in the Folder List pane.

◆ To open a Web page in *another* Web site, choose File > Open and then use the dialog box that appears to navigate to the desired page.

To change a page's name:

1. Click the file in the Folder List to select it. Wait a beat and click it again to select its name (**Figure 3.24**).

2. Use your cursor to select everything but the .htm suffix (left, **Figure 3.25**). Type a new name (right, **Figure 3.25**). Press (←Enter).

   The new name is applied to the file (**Figure 3.26**).

Figure 3.24 Click once, wait a beat, and click again to select the file's name in the Folder List.

Figure 3.25 Select everything but the .htm suffix (left), then type a new name (right).

Figure 3.26 Press (←Enter) and the new name is applied to the file.

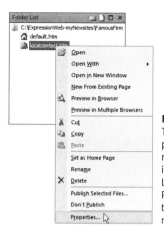

Figure 3.27
To change a
page's title,
right-click a page
in the Folder
List and choose
Properties from
the drop-down
menu.

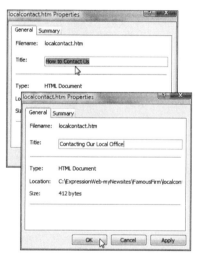

Figure 3.28 Select the title in the General
tab (top), type a new title, and click OK to
apply the change and close the dialog box
(bottom).

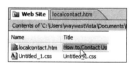

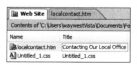

Figure 3.29 If the
Title column is
turned on in the
Editing Window,
you can select the
title there and type
a new title.

To change a page's title:

1. Right-click a page in the Folder List, and choose Properties from the drop-down menu (**Figure 3.27**).

2. Select the title in the General tab of the Properties dialog box (top, **Figure 3.28**). Type a new title and click OK to apply the change and close the dialog box (bottom, **Figure 3.28**).

✔ Tip

■ If the Title column is turned on in the Editing Window (click Reports tab > All Files), you can select the title in the column and type in a new title (**Figure 3.29**).

CHANGING A PAGE'S TITLE

To delete a Web page:

1. In the Folder List, right-click the page and choose Delete from the drop-down menu (**Figure 3.30**).

2. An alert dialog box appears, asking if you want to delete the page (**Figure 3.31**). Click Yes, and the page is deleted from the site.

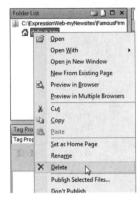

Figure 3.30 To delete a page, right-click it in the Folder List and choose Delete from the drop-down menu.

Figure 3.31 If you're sure you want to delete the page, click Yes.

DELETING A WEB PAGE

Setting Other Page Properties

Besides enabling you to change a page's title, the Page Properties dialog box controls many other aspects of individual pages. You can set a page's background image, sound, and color. You also can change the color of your text and link colors—though you're much better off using CSS to set those aspects (see "Creating Styles with CSS" on page 123).

To set page properties:

1. Open the page you want to change, and choose File > Properties.

   When the Page Properties dialog box appears, the General tab opens by default.

2. Click the tab you want to use, and select the options you want to set within that tab.

3. After making your choices, click OK to close the dialog and apply the property changes.

4. Save the page (Ctrl S). If you add an image or sound file that's not already part of the site, click OK when the Save Embedded Files dialog box appears. To see the result in your main Web browser, press F12.

Page Properties

Of the five tabs in the Page Properties dialog box, General and Formatting get the most use.

◆ **General** controls the title (as explained on page 43) (**Figure 3.32**). The Page description and Keywords fields harken back to the days when search engines used this metadata to categorize your pages. Nowadays, such engines just search the body of your pages, but these two items remain useful for pages you're migrating from FrontPage to Expression Web. If you want to use a Background sound, click that pane's Browse button to navigate to the sound file. Do not use the Location path to move a page; just click and drag it in the Folder List.

◆ **Formatting** controls the background image, plus the color of the text and hyperlinks. To add a background image, select Background picture; select Make it a watermark if you want the image to be semitransparent (top, **Figure 3.33**). Browse to the image you want to use, and after you select an image, the Formatting tab lists the image's path (bottom, **Figure 3.33**). (To remove the image, select the path and click Delete.) To change the background, text, or link colors of a single page, use the bottom Colors pane of the Page Properties dialog box.

Figure 3.32 Use the General tab in the Page Properties dialog box to set the title, page description, keywords, and background sound.

Figure 3.33 Use the Formatting tab in the Page Properties dialog box to set the background image, plus the colors of the background, text, and links.

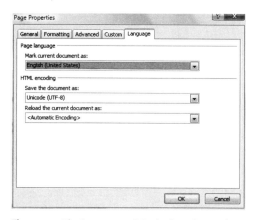

Figure 3.34 The Language tab in the Page Properties dialog box sets the language and encoding options.

◆ **Advanced** lets you set the margins for that particular page, but again, it's best to handle this using CSS (see "Creating Layouts with CSS" on page 147)

◆ **Custom** lets you create custom code snippets based on system and user variables.

◆ **Language** controls both the page's language and HTML encoding (**Figure 3.34**). Together, they ensure that Expression Web and your browser use the appropriate character sets for the language being used. In general, however, this usually is handled by your computer's main settings.

✔ Tip

■ The Workgroup feature was discontinued in Expression Web 2.

Previewing Pages in a Browser

Expression Web's Design view does a pretty good job of showing how your Web pages will appear once published. But you should make a habit of previewing the page in a variety of Web browsers to spot inconsistencies from browser to browser. By adding multiple browsers to Expression Web's built-in preview list, you can quickly switch from one preview to another. Windows Vista does not support pre-7.0 versions of Internet Explorer, so you'll need an Windows XP machine to preview pages in IE 6 and earlier. It's a bother but worth the effort since it'll likely take several years before most visitors upgrade to Vista and IE 7.

To preview pages:

◆ Save any changes to your page (Ctrl S). Choose File > Preview in Browser and make a choice in the drop-down menu (left, **Figure 3.35**). Or do the same with the Preview button in the Common toolbar (right, **Figure 3.35**). The selected browser launches and displays the selected Web page.

✔ Tips

■ To designate any browser in the list as your default choice, press Shift as you select it in the drop-down menu. You can then trigger a preview by that browser at any time by pressing F12. To designate another browser as the default, repeat the Shift-click in the list.

■ You also can preview any page by right-clicking it in the Folder List and choosing Preview in Browser from the drop-down menu.

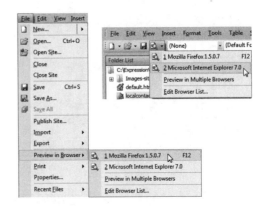

Figure 3.35 To see any saved page in your Web browser, choose File > Preview in Browser and make a choice in the drop-down menu (left) or click the Preview button in the Common toolbar (right).

Figure 3.36 To include another Web browser in your list, click Add.

Figure 3.37 Click Browse to navigate to the browser program you want to add (top). Once you add the program, the dialog box reappears listing the path to the program. Type a shorthand name and version in the Name box, and click OK (bottom).

Figure 3.38 The additional program appears in the list. Checked browsers automatically open whenever you choose Preview in Multiple Browsers (shown in Figure 3.35).

To change the Web browser list:

1. Choose File > Preview in Browser > Edit Browser List, or click the Common toolbar's Preview button and choose Edit Browser List.

2. Click Add in the Edit Browser List (**Figure 3.36**).

3. In the Add Browser dialog box, click Browse to navigate to the browser program you want to add (top, **Figure 3.37**).

4. Once you find the program and click Open, the Add Browser dialog box reappears listing the path to the program. Type a shorthand name and version into the Name box, and click OK (bottom, **Figure 3.37**).

5. When the Edit Browser List dialog box reappears, the browser is added to the list. Click OK to close the box and apply the changes (**Figure 3.38**). For the dialog box's other options, see the Tips below.

✔ Tips

- In step 4, select Automatically save page before previewing to have Expression Web automatically save your work before you preview pages (**Figure 3.38**).

- In step 4, select any of the three Additional window sizes to add them to the Preview drop-down menu choices (**Figure 3.38**).

- You can see a page previewed in multiple browsers simultaneously. In step 4, just select the checkboxes next to any of the listed browsers (**Figure 3.38**). To trigger the multiple displays, choose Preview in Multiple Browsers in the Preview drop-down menu (**Figure 3.35**).

PREVIEWING PAGES IN A BROWSER

49

WORKING WITH TEXT

On the surface, working with text in Expression Web is very much like using any word processing program. Unlike with word processing, however, you should not format your Web text (bold, italic, font size, and so on) as you enter it. It's true that in the early days of the Web, you often applied font and style tags in the same as-you-worked fashion as word processing. Modern Web standards, however, try as much as possible to separate what the text says (its content) from how it looks (its appearance or presentation).

That's in part because a Web page may be read on a cell phone screen or a page-sized monitor. By separating content from presentation, it's much easier to create codes that allow your Web pages to automatically adjust to whatever reads them (including text-to-speech programs for the visually impaired).

Think instead of your text and headings as you would an outline. Outlines seldom look fancy. Instead, they focus on the sequence and relative importance of different parts of your information by using headings and indents. For that reason, this chapter shows you how to treat your text more like an outline. As for the business of formatting the appearance of your text, see "Creating Styles with CSS" on page 123.

Entering and Selecting Text

The standard techniques you use in text-editing programs—entering text, selecting, moving, cutting, and copying—work similarly in Expression Web.

To enter text on a Web page:

1. Open the Web page in which you want to work, and click where you want to enter text.

   A blinking vertical bar marks the text insertion spot.

2. Start typing, and the text appears at the insertion spot (**Figure 4.1**).

✔ Tip

■ Notice in the code window that Expression Web automatically places the text inside an HTML paragraph tag (<p> </p>) (**Figure 4.1**). Called a *container*, this tag offers a stripped-down example of how HTML works: An opening tag marks (declares) the start of a particular code effect, and a closing tags marks where it ends. As you dive deeper into Expression Web, you'll see how all HTML and CSS coding works the same way.

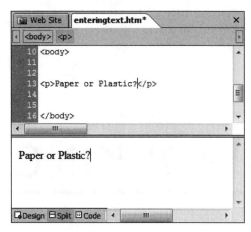

Figure 4.1 To enter text on a Web page, start typing and the text appears at the insertion spot.

To select text on a page:

Do one of the following:

◆ Click and drag through the text you want to select.

◆ Double-click a word to select it.

◆ Triple-click anywhere in a paragraph to select it.

◆ Click at the beginning (or end) of the text you want to select, and press [Ctrl][Shift][→] (or [Ctrl][Shift][←]) until you've selected all the desired text.

◆ Move your cursor to the left end of a line, and when it becomes an arrow, click to select the entire line.

◆ Move your cursor to the left end of a line, and when it becomes an arrow, double-click to select the entire paragraph.

To move text:

1. Select the text you want to move (**Figure 4.2**).

2. Click and drag the highlighted text to its new location (**Figure 4.3**).

3. Release your cursor, and the selected text moves to the new spot (**Figure 4.4**).

To cut or copy text:

1. Select the text you want to cut or copy.

2. Choose Edit > Cut ([Ctrl][X]), or right-click and choose Cut from the drop-down menu.

    The selected text is stored in the Clipboard for pasting elsewhere.

    or

    Choose Edit > Copy ([Ctrl][C]), or right-click and choose Copy from the drop-down menu.

    The selected text is stored in the Clipboard for pasting elsewhere.

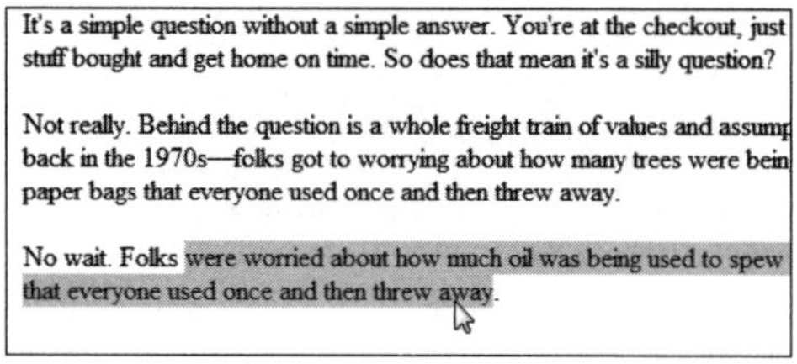

Figure 4.2 Select the text you want to move.

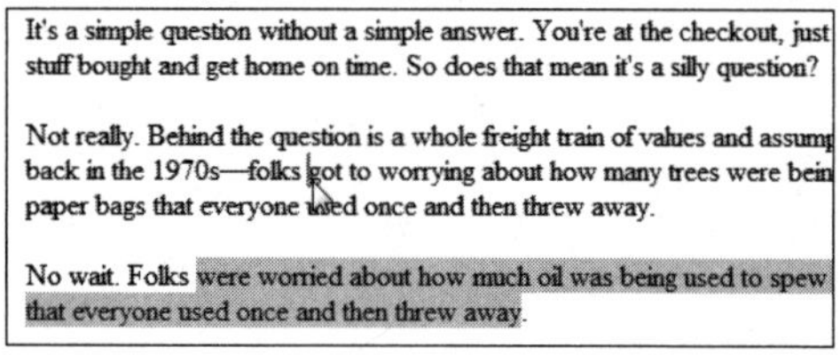

Figure 4.3 Click and drag the highlighted text to its new location.

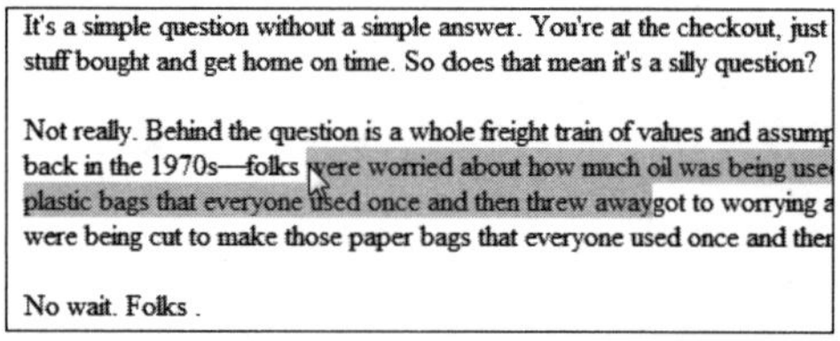

Figure 4.4 Release the cursor, and the selected text moves to the new spot.

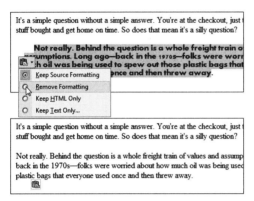

Figure 4.5 If you don't want to keep the formatting of the source document, right-click the Paste Options button.

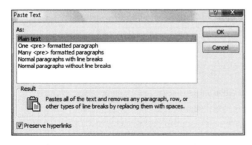

Figure 4.6 Choose Remove Formatting in the drop-down menu (top) to match the formatting of the destination document (bottom).

Figure 4.7 To control line breaks and white space in the inserted text, choose Edit > Paste Text.

Figure 4.8 When the Paste Text dialog box appears, pick one of the five choices. (See Table 4.2.)

Pasting Text

Expression Web gives you two ways to paste text, each of which controls a different aspect. The commonly used Paste command (Ctrl V) includes options for controlling the *style* of the inserted text. Expression Web's Paste Text command, which has no keyboard shortcut, includes options for controlling the *line breaks* and *white space* of the inserted text.

To paste text:

1. Make sure you're in Design view. Click in the page where you want to insert text that you've cut from a Web page or from another program, such as Microsoft Word.

2. Choose Edit > Paste (Ctrl V), or right-click and choose Paste.

   The stored text is pasted into the *destination* document at the insertion point and, by default, retains the formatting of the *source* document from where it's cut or copied. If you don't want to keep the formatting, right-click the Paste Options button that appears amid the inserted text (**Figure 4.5**). Choose Remove Formatting in the drop-down menu to match the formatting of the destination document (**Figure 4.6**). For more information, see "Controlling Paste Styles" on page 56.)

   or

   Choose Edit > Paste Text (**Figure 4.7**). When the Paste Text dialog box appears, pick one of the five choices (**Figure 4.8**).

   The text is pasted based on your choice. For more information, see "Controlling Paste Line Breaks and White Space" on page 56.

   (continued)

PASTING TEXT

✔ Tips

- The Remove Formatting choice is very handy when, for example, you're copying text from a Web page full of pre-CSS font tags.

- The Paste Text dialog box's no-line-breaks choice saves time when copying multiline text from tables into a page without tables.

- If the text you're pasting from another page has a format style that uses the *exact name* as your destination page, the Paste Options drop-down menu includes the option of matching the *destination* page's style (**Figure 4.9**).

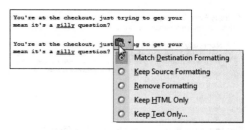

Figure 4.9 If the *source* text includes a style with the same name as your destination page, the drop-down menu includes the option of matching the *destination* page's style.

Table 4.1

Controlling Paste Styles	
CHOOSE	TO
Match Destination Formatting	Preserve formatting of the *destination* page
Keep Source Formatting	Preserve formatting of the *source* document
Remove Formatting	Insert plain text
Keep HTML Only	Preserve HTML coding copied from the source
Keep Text Only	Insert plain text—same as Remove Formatting—except the Paste Text dialog box appears, letting you control line breaks and white space (See Table 4.2 below.)

Table 4.2

Controlling Paste Line Breaks and White Space	
CHOOSE	TO
Plain text	Insert plain text with spaces replacing any line breaks in source text
One <pre> formatted paragraph	Use <pre> (preformatted) tag to maintain all line breaks of source text
Many <pre> formatted paragraphs	Use <pre> tag to maintain all line and paragraph breaks of source text
Normal paragraphs with line breaks	Convert any lines breaks to (line break) tag and any paragraph breaks to <p> (paragraph) tag
Normal paragraphs without line breaks	Do exactly that

Figure 4.10 The Undo and Redo drop-down menus in the Standard toolbar let you choose how many actions to step backward or forward.

To undo an action:

◆ Choose Edit > Undo, or press Ctrl Z.
   The previous action is undone.

To redo an action:

◆ Choose Edit > Redo, or press Ctrl Y.
   The previous action is reapplied.

✔ Tips

■ The Undo and Redo choices change in the Edit menu depending on your previous actions.

■ If the Standard toolbar is visible, you can use the drop-down menus of the Undo or Redo buttons to choose how many actions you want step backward or forward (**Figure 4.10**).

To add a line break:

Do one of the following:

◆ Click your cursor where you want the text to break, and press [Shift][←Enter].

The text breaks to a new line.

◆ Click your cursor where you want the text to break, and choose Insert > HTML > Break (**Figure 4.11**).

The text breaks to a new line.

◆ Click your cursor where you want the text to break, and in the Toolbox task pane, look in the HTML-Tags section and double-click the Break button (**Figure 4.12**).

The text breaks to a new line.

To add a paragraph break:

◆ Click in the text where you want a new paragraph to begin, and press [←Enter].

The cursor or text jumps to the next line to start a new paragraph.

To show/hide line break and paragraph marks:

◆ Click the Show All button in the Standard toolbar (**Figure 4.13**). All the normally hidden line break and paragraph marks appear. To hide the marks, click the Show All button again.

Just as you can show/hide various toolbars or task panes, click the arrow next to the Show All button and use the drop-down menu to turn on/off ten different categories of marks (**Figure 4.14**).

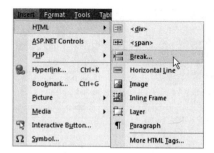

Figure 4.11 To add a line break, choose Insert > HTML > Break.

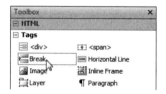

Figure 4.12 You also can double-click the Break button in the Toolbox task pane.

Figure 4.13 To show line break and paragraph marks, click the Show All button in the Standard toolbar. Click again to hide them.

Figure 4.14 You can click the arrow next to the Show All button's and use the drop-down menu to turn on/off ten categories of marks.

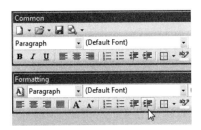

Figure 4.15 The Increase Indent Position button appears in the Common and Formatting toolbars.

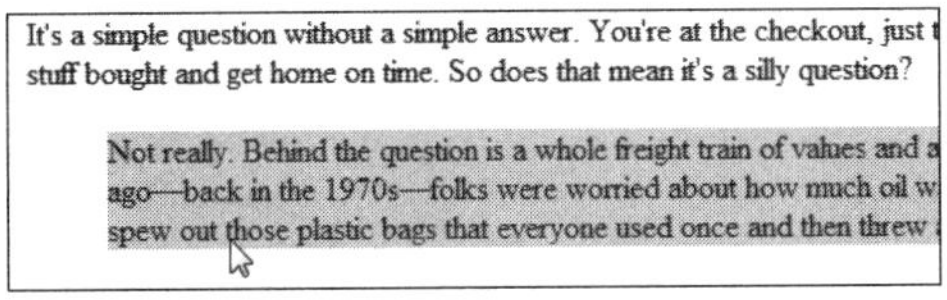

It's a simple question without a simple answer. You're at the checkout, just t stuff bought and get home on time. So does that mean it's a silly question?

Not really. Behind the question is a whole freight train of values and a ago—back in the 1970s—folks were worried about how much oil w spew out those plastic bags that everyone used once and then threw a

Figure 4.16 The selected paragraph indents by 40 pixels.

Indenting Paragraphs

Indenting offers a quick way to structure your text since indented items signal that they are less important, or at least a subset, of the less-indented item above. It's no wonder that indenting plays a big role in creating outlines, which like Web pages focus on the structure of the information rather than its appearance. Not to worry: Using CSS you can control precisely how indented text looks. But it's a separate process covered in "Creating Styles with CSS" on page 123. Here, we just show you how to apply a basic indent.

To indent paragraph:

1. Click anywhere in a single paragraph (or click and drag to select multiple paragraphs).

2. Press [Tab] or the Increase Indent Position button in the Common or Formatting toolbars (**Figure 4.15**).

   The selected paragraph(s) indents (**Figure 4.16**). To further indent the text, click the button again.

✔ Tip

- Use the adjacent Decrease Indent Position button to reduce the indent.

To indent a paragraph's first line:

1. Click anywhere in the paragraph, and choose Format > Paragraph (**Figure 4.17**).
2. In the Paragraph dialog box, type a number in the Indent first line field or use the small arrows to select a number (**Figure 4.18**).

   The bottom Preview area shows the effect.
3. When you're satisfied, click OK to close the dialog box and apply the indent (**Figure 4.19**).

Format
Tools
Table
Site
Data View
New Style...
CSS Styles
CSS Properties...
Tag Properties...
Font...
Paragraph...
Bullets and Numbering...
Borders and Shading...

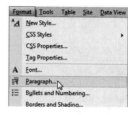

Figure 4.17 To indent just a paragraph's first line, choose Format > Paragraph.

Paragraph
Indents and Spacing
Alignment:
Default
Indentation
Left side:
0
Right side:
0
Indent first line:
60
Spacing
Before:
After:
Word:
Line spacing:
Preview

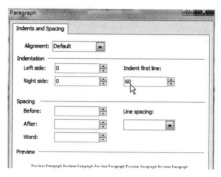

Figure 4.18 In the Paragraph dialog box, type a number in the Indent first line field. The Preview area at the bottom shows the effect.

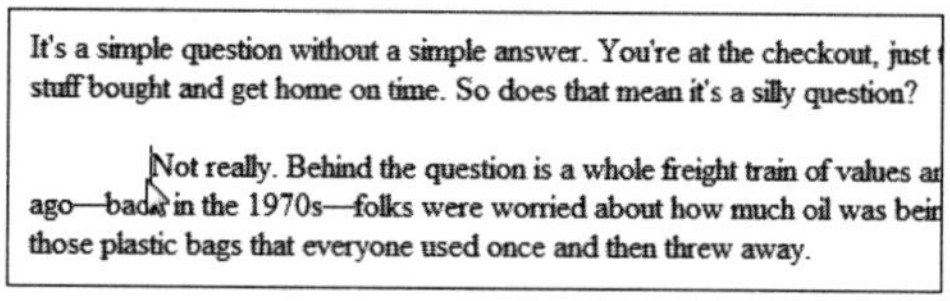

It's a simple question without a simple answer. You're at the checkout, just
stuff bought and get home on time. So does that mean it's a silly question?
Not really. Behind the question is a whole freight train of values a
ago—back in the 1970s—folks were worried about how much oil was bei
those plastic bags that everyone used once and then threw away.

Figure 4.19 The first line of the selected paragraph indents by the amount you select.

Figure 4.20 To align text, choose one of the alignment buttons in the Common or Formatting toolbars.

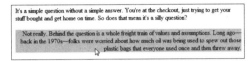

Figure 4.21 The selected paragraph changes to a centered alignment.

Aligning Text

Much like a word-processing program, Expression Web can align selected text to the left, the right, or center it. It also can justify the text, though that's less commonly used on the Web.

To align text:

◆ Click anywhere in a single paragraph (or click and drag to select multiple paragraphs), and click one of the alignment buttons in the Common or Formatting toolbars (**Figure 4.20**).

The selected paragraphs realign based on your choice (**Figure 4.21**).

✔ Tip

■ Unlike the Common toolbar, the Formatting toolbar includes a Justify button. Take care, however, that the Justify button doesn't spread out your words so much that you wind up with unsightly gaps in some of the paragraph lines.

Inserting Special HTML Characters

HTML by necessity uses special codes to create the sort of special characters taken for granted in word processing.

To insert a special character:

1. Click in the text where you want to insert the special character, and choose Insert > Symbol (**Figure 4.22**).

2. In the Symbol dialog box, use the Font and Subset drop-down menus to find the character you need (**Figure 4.23**). Or make a selection in the Recently used symbols bar. Click the character to select it, and choose Insert.

   The correct HTML code for the character is inserted into your text.

✔ Tips

■ If you're looking for such common punctuation marks as dashes or ellipses, in step 2 use the General Punctuation Subset drop-down menu (**Figure 4.23**).

■ Over time, your most-used characters will fill the Recently used symbols bar, reducing the need to dig through the Font and Subset drop-down menus.

Figure 4.22 Click in the text where you want to insert the special character, and choose Insert > Symbol.

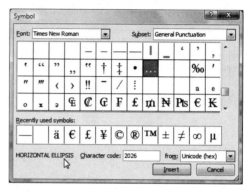

Figure 4.23 Use the Font and Subset drop-down menus to find the character you need. Or make a selection in the Recently used symbols bar.

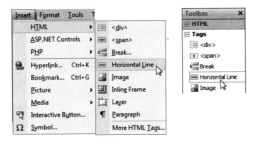

Figure 4.24 To insert a horizontal line, choose Insert > HTML > Horizontal Line (left) or click the Horizontal Line button in the Toolbox task pane (right).

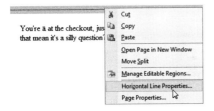

Figure 4.25 To change a line's properties, right-click it and choose Horizontal Line Properties in the drop-down menu.

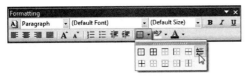

Figure 4.26
Use the Horizontal Line Properties dialog box to change the line's width, height, alignment, and color.

To insert a horizontal line:

◆ Click in the text where you want to add the line, and choose Insert > HTML > Horizontal Line (left, **Figure 4.24**), or if the Toolbox task pane is open, you can click the Horizontal Line button found under HTML > Tags (right, **Figure 4.24**). The line appears on the page.

✔ Tips

■ To change the line's properties, right-click the line and choose Horizontal Line Properties from the drop-down menu (**Figure 4.25**). Use the Horizontal Line Properties dialog box to change the width (best done as a percent of the window rather than an absolute value) (**Figure 4.26**). You also can change the line's height, alignment, and color. Click OK to apply the changes.

■ If the Formatting toolbar is visible, you'll also find a horizontal line button in the drop-down menu for the Outside Borders button (**Figure 4.27**).

Figure 4.27 In the Formatting toolbar you'll also find a horizontal line button in the drop-down menu for the Outside Borders button.

Creating Headings

In some ways, headings are your most important tool for guiding readers through your Web pages. While paragraph-level text supplies the content of your pages, it's the headings that give it structure. Properly functioning headings enable readers to scan a page for a particular topic—without needing to read any of the text details.

HTML offers six sizes of headings, with h1 being the largest and h6 the smallest. None of the sizes come with a fixed value. Think instead of h1–h6 headings as a way to clue the reader about the *relative* importance of one item to another. Save h1 for your most important headings, for example, such as the tops of pages. H2 and h3 then might be used for subheadings, while h4 or h5 might mark sections in your sidebars. The main thing: Be consistent in using the sizes to structure your content. As for making your headings black or red, serif or sans serif, that's best done using CSS, as explained in "Creating Styles with CSS" on page 123.

To create a heading:

1. Click anywhere in the text you want to make into a heading (**Figure 4.28**).

2. Click the Style drop-down menu in the Common or Formatting toolbar, and choose a heading size (**Figure 4.29**).
   The heading is applied to the text (**Figure 4.30**).

✔ Tips

■ Headings apply to the whole paragraph, so put the heading in its own short paragraph of no more than two short lines. Even shorter is better.

■ In step 2 if you change your mind about your size choice, just select another choice in the Style drop-down menu and it is applied instead.

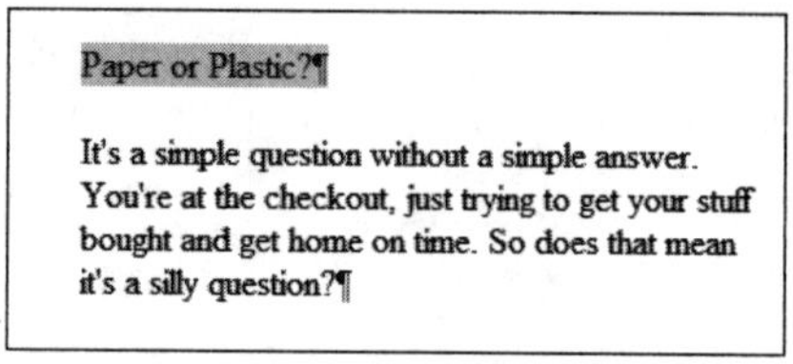

Paper or Plastic?¶

It's a simple question without a simple answer. You're at the checkout, just trying to get your stuff bought and get home on time. So does that mean it's a silly question?¶

Figure 4.28 Click anywhere in the line you want to make into a heading.

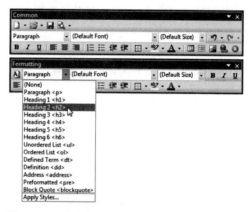

Figure 4.29 Click the Style drop-down menu in the Common or Formatting toolbar to choose a heading size.

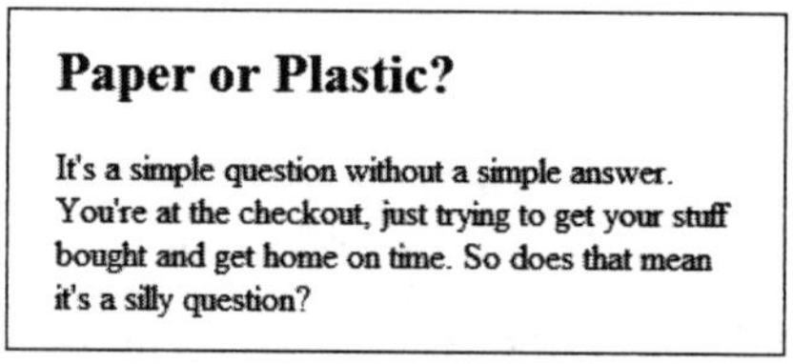

Paper or Plastic?

It's a simple question without a simple answer. You're at the checkout, just trying to get your stuff bought and get home on time. So does that mean it's a silly question?

Figure 4.30 The selected line turns into an h2-sized heading.

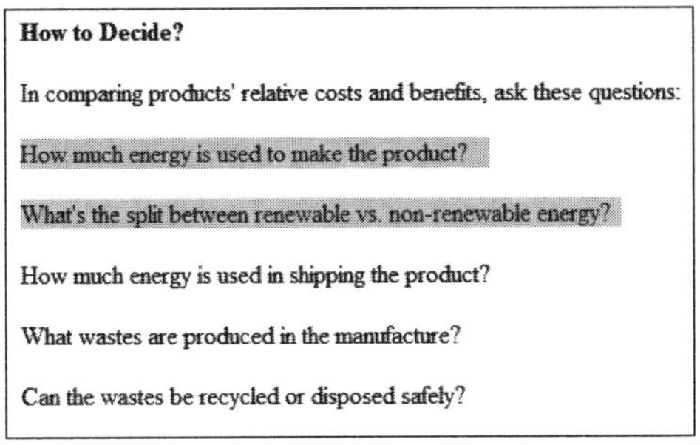

How to Decide?
In comparing products' relative costs and benefits, ask these questions:
How much energy is used to make the product?
What's the split between renewable vs. non-renewable energy?
How much energy is used in shipping the product?
What wastes are produced in the manufacture?
Can the wastes be recycled or disposed safely?

Figure 4.31 Select the lines you want numbered.

Formatting
Paragraph
(Default Font)
(Default Size)
Common
Paragraph
(Default Font)
(Default Size)

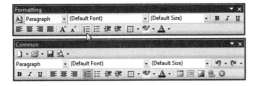

Figure 4.32 Click the Numbering button in either the Formatting or Common toolbar.

How to Decide?
In comparing products' relative costs and benefits, ask these questions:
1. How much energy is used to make the product?
2. What's the split between renewable vs. non-renewable energy?
How much energy is used in shipping the product?
What wastes are produced in the manufacture?
Can the wastes be recycled or disposed safely?

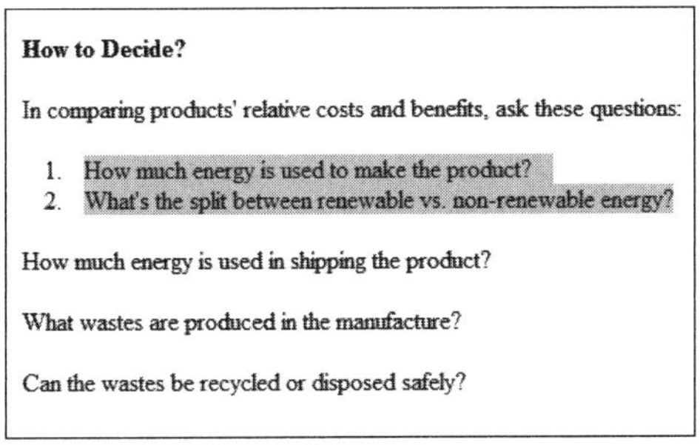

Figure 4.33 The lines are indented and numbered.

Creating Lists

Lists come in two flavors: ordered (numbered) and unordered (bulleted). You can change the defaults Expression Web uses for lists (letters instead of numbers, square bullets instead of round ones). For anything fancier, however, you're better off using CSS to create sitewide styles for such lists. For more information, see "Creating Styles with CSS" on page 123.

To create a numbered list:

1. Select the lines you want numbered (**Figure 4.31**).
2. Click the Numbering button in either the Formatting or Common toolbar (**Figure 4.32**).

   The lines are indented and numbered (**Figure 4.33**).

To create a bulleted list:

1. Select the lines you want bulleted (**Figure 4.34**).

2. Click the Bullets button in either the Formatting or Common toolbar (**Figure 4.35**).

   The lines are indented and bulleted (**Figure 4.36**).

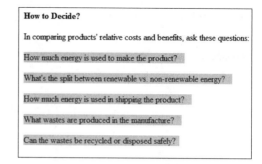

Figure 4.34 Select the lines you want bulleted.

Figure 4.35 Click the Bullets button in either the Formatting or Common toolbar.

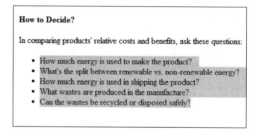

Figure 4.36 The lines are indented and bulleted.

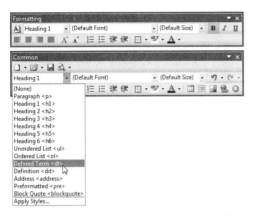

Figure 4.37 Place your cursor where you want the first definition to appear, and then choose Defined Term from the Style drop-down menu in the Formatting or Common toolbar.

Figure 4.38 The Quick Tag Selector at the top of the Editing Window tells you that the line is tagged as a defined term.

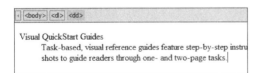

Figure 4.39 Press ⏎Enter, and the next block of text is formatted as the definition of the term above it.

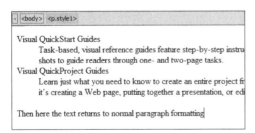

Figure 4.40 When you're done adding terms, press ⏎Enter twice and the text returns to the normal paragraph formatting.

To create a definition list:

1. Place your cursor where you want the first definition to appear.

2. Use the Style drop-down menu in the Formatting or Common toolbar to choose Defined Term (**Figure 4.37**).

3. Type your first term (**Figure 4.38**).

4. Press ⏎Enter, and the text is indented and formatted as the definition of the term above it (**Figure 4.39**).

5. When you finished entering the definition, if you want to add more terms, press ⏎Enter again and the cursor jumps to a new line and switches back to the Defined Term format.

6. When you're done adding terms, press ⏎Enter twice and Expression Web switches back to the normal body text (**Figure 4.40**).

✔ Tip

■ You can type all the terms and definitions and then format them line by line using the Style drop-down menu. But it's generally easier to switch to the Defined Term format and type them all at once since all the formatting is handled automatically.

To end a list:

◆ To add more items to your list—whether numbered, bulleted, or definition—press ⏎Enter *once* and the cursor starts a fresh, indented line where you may continue typing (top, **Figure 4.41**). When you're done and want to return to the regular paragraph formatting, press ⏎Enter *twice*. The cursor skips a line and is no longer indented (bottom, **Figure 4.41**).

To remove list formatting:

1. Select a single or multiple lines from which you want to remove numbering or bullets.

2. If the list is numbered, click the Numbering button in either the Formatting or Common toolbar.

   The number formatting is removed.

   or

   If the list is bulleted, click the Bullets button in either the Formatting or Common toolbar.

   The bullet formatting is removed.

How to Decide?

1. In comparing products' relative costs and benefits,
2. How much energy is used to make the product?
3. What's the split between renewable vs. non-renew
4. How much energy is used in shipping the product?
5. What wastes are produced in the manufacture?
6. Can the wastes be recycled or disposed safely?
7. |

How to Decide?

1. In comparing products' relative costs and benefits,
2. How much energy is used to make the product?
3. What's the split between renewable vs. non-renew
4. How much energy is used in shipping the product?
5. What wastes are produced in the manufacture?
6. Can the wastes be recycled or disposed safely?

|

Figure 4.41 To add more items to the list, press ⏎Enter *once* and the cursor starts a fresh, indented line (top). To return to the regular paragraph formatting, press ⏎Enter *twice* (bottom).

How to Decide?

In comparing products' relative costs and benefits, ask these questions:

1. How much energy is used to make the product?
2. What's the split between renewable vs. non-renewable energy?
3. How much energy is used in shipping the product?
4. What wastes are produced in the manufacture?
5. Can the wastes be recycled or disposed safely?

Figure 4.42 Click at the end of the line in your list where you want to create a sublist.

1. How much energy is used to make the product?
2. What's the split between renewable vs. non-renewable energy?
3. How much energy is used in shipping the product?
   1. |
4. What wastes are produced in the manufacture?

Figure 4.43 Press ⏎Enter, and then press Tab to start a sublist with the same formatting as the parent list.

1. How much energy is used to make the product?
2. What's the split between renewable vs. non-renewable energy?
3. How much energy is used in shipping the product?
   1. Are there choices in shipping method?
   2. Can you bundled together shipments?
   3. Do local suppliers use less energy for shipments?
4. What wastes are produced in the manufacture?

Figure 4.44 Add items to the sublist by pressing ⏎Enter when you need to add a new line.

3. How much energy is used in shipping the product?
   1. Are there choices in shipping method?
   2. Can you bundled together shipments?
   3. Do local suppliers use less energy for shipments?
4. What wastes are produced in the manufacture?
5. Can the wastes be recycled or disposed safely?

Figure 4.45 To add items to the main list, click at the end and press ⏎Enter.

3. How much energy is used in shipping the product?
   1. Are there choices in shipping method?
   2. Can you bundled together shipments?
   3. Do local suppliers use less energy for shipments?
4. What wastes are produced in the manufacture?
5. Can the wastes be recycled or disposed safely?
6. |

Figure 4.46 A new, nonnested item is added to the list.

To create a nested sublist:

1. Click at the end of the line in your list where you want to create a sublist, sometimes called a nested list (**Figure 4.42**).

2. Press ⏎Enter, and then press Tab. Expression Web starts a new sublist using the same list formatting as the parent list (**Figure 4.43**).

3. Add items to the sublist, pressing ⏎Enter when you need to add a new line (**Figure 4.44**). (To reformat the sublist, see "To reformat lists" on the next page.)

4. When you finish adding to the sublist, click anywhere back in the main list. To add items to the main list, click at the end and press ⏎Enter to resume (**Figure 4.45**).

   A new, nonnested item is added to the list (**Figure 4.46**).

To reformat lists:

1. Select the list lines you want to reformat (**Figure 4.47**).

2. Choose Format > Bullets and Numbering (**Figure 4.48**).

   The List Properties dialog box automatically displays the tab whose format matches the selection.

3. Pick a format, or click one of the other tabs to find what you want (**Figure 4.49**).

4. Click OK, and the selected lines are reformatted (**Figure 4.50**).

✔ Tips

- Reformatting leaves any *nested* lists in their original format (**Figure 4.51**).

- While the List Properties dialog box includes an option to use your own customized picture bullets, you'll have more flexibility if you leave the tab set to Use current CSS style (**Figure 4.52**). That way you can create and update custom bullets across your site. For more information, see "Creating Styles with CSS" on page 123.

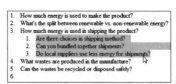

Figure 4.47 Select the list lines you want to reformat.

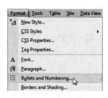

Figure 4.48 Choose Format > Bullets and Numbering.

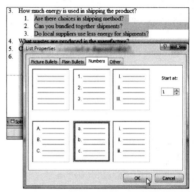

Figure 4.49 In the List Properties dialog box, pick a format or click one of the other tabs to find what you want.

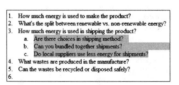

Figure 4.50 The selected lines are reformatted based on your choice in the List Properties dialog box.

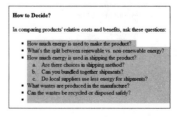

Figure 4.51 Reformatting preserves any *nested* lists in their original format.

Figure 4.52 While the List Properties dialog box lets you use customized picture bullets, you'll have more flexibility if you leave the tab set to Use current CSS style.

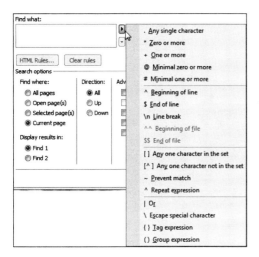

Figure 4.53 In the Find and Replace dialog box, you can use the Find what field's drop-down menu or type in your own text.

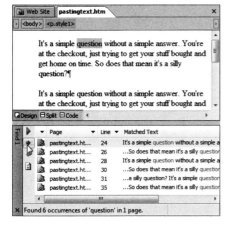

Figure 4.54 The search item is highlighted in the page (top). Click the Next button to move through the page.

Searching Text, Code, or Tags

Beyond the standard find and replace functions, you'd expect, Expression Web also lets you search and replace bits of your code across an entire Web site. That can be especially handy when trying to track down problems. The Find and Replace dialog box's many options make it easy to zero in on even the tiniest bit of code across the largest of sites. It also includes an option to search and change just HTML tags.

To find text or code on a single page:

1. To search a single page, open it or select it in the Folder List.

2. Choose Edit > Find (Ctrl F).

3. In the Find and Replace dialog box, type what you're searching for in the Find what field or click the field's drop-down menu and choose an appropriate item (**Figure 4.53**).

4. Use the Search options pane to specify where to look, the direction of the search, or such things as the case of the item.

5. If you click Find Next, the search item is highlighted (**Figure 4.54**). The page remains visible, enabling you to use the Find Next button to move through the page.

   or

   If you click Find All, the first instance of the search item is highlighted in the page and the Find and Replace dialog box is replaced by the Find pane listing all the instances found. Click the Find pane's blue Next or Back arrows to continue searching the page. To close the Find pane, click the X in the pane's title bar.

✔ Tip

■ The Split view lets you search for text or code without having to change your view.

To find text or code across the site:

1. Open the site you want to search, and select its name in the Folder List (**Figure 4.55**).

2. Choose Edit > Find.

3. In the Find and Replace dialog box, type in the Find what box the term you're searching for or use the field's drop-down menu to choose an appropriate item. If necessary, use the Advanced pane to further hone the search. Click Find All (**Figure 4.56**).

   A Find pane lists the search results by page, line number, and context (**Figure 4.57**).

4. Click the Find pane's blue Next result arrow, and Expression Web automatically opens the page containing the search term and highlights it in context (**Figure 4.58**).

5. Click the Find pane's blue Next result arrow to see the next instance of the search term, or click the blue Back arrow to see the previous instance. To close the Find pane, click the X in the pane's title bar.

✔ Tips

- Since you selected the entire site in step 1, the Find where options in step 2 are ignored (**Figure 4.56**).

- In step 4, any pages not already open are displayed automatically in the view last used for that page, whether it's Design, Split, or Code.

- You can search multiple pages without searching the entire site. In step 1, [Ctrl]-click the pages in the Folder List that you want to search and follow the rest of the steps from there.

Figure 4.55 To search an entire site, select its name in the Folder List.

Figure 4.56 Type in the Find what box the term you're searching for, use the Advanced pane to further hone the search, and click Find All.

Figure 4.57 A Find pane lists the search results by page, line number, and context.

Figure 4.58 Click the Find pane's Next arrow, and the page containing the term opens automatically.

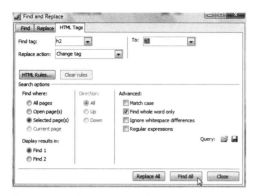

Figure 4.59 In the HTML Tags tab, set up what you want to find and replace using the Find tag, Replace action, and To drop-down menus.

Figure 4.60 When the Find pane displays the search results, look through the Matched Text column to see if Expression Web found what you wanted.

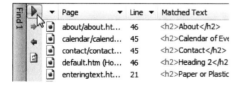

Figure 4.61 Click the arrow at the top of the Find pane to return to the Find and Replace dialog box.

To find and replace HTML tags:

1. In the Folder List, select the entire site, single page, or multiple pages (using [Ctrl]-click) in which you want to find a particular HTML tag, and choose Edit > Find.

2. In the Find and Replace dialog box, select the HTML Tags tab. Set up what you want to find and replace using the Find tag, Replace action, and To drop-down menus (**Figure 4.59**).

3. If you want, use the Find where section of the Search options pane to expand or narrow the pages searched and the Advanced section to further hone the search. Since Expression Web cannot undo a replace-all action, click Find All (not Replace All).

4. When the Find pane displays the search results, look through the Matched Text column to see if Expression Web found what you wanted. If you have any doubts, select the page listing and click the blue Next result arrow (**Figure 4.60**). The page opens so that you can get a better look.

5. Once you've taken a good look at the results, click the *green* arrow at the top of the Find pane (**Figure 4.61**).

    The Find and Replace dialog box reappears.

(continued)

6. (Optional) If necessary, you can adjust the find and replace actions and then, if you're being extra careful, select Find 2 in the Display results in section (**Figure 4.62**). Click Find All again, and a second tab appears in the Find pane (**Figure 4.63**). Switch between the two tabs to compare the results. Repeat step 5 to return to the Find and Replace dialog box until you're satisfied with the results. Then return to the Find and Replace dialog box one last time.

7. Click Replace All in the Find and Replace dialog box (**Figure 4.64**). Assuming you've doubled-checked your work, click Yes when the alert dialog box appears (**Figure 4.65**).

Expression Web makes the replacements and lists the actions in the Find pane (**Figure 4.66**).

✔ Tips

- If you're familiar with regular expressions and wild card searches, that option's available in the Advanced section of the Find and Replace dialog box.

- Click the HTML Rules button in the Find and Replace dialog box if you want to add customized rules for searching.

Figure 4.62 You can adjust the find and replace actions and display the results in a new pane by selecting Find 2.

Figure 4.63 By switching the Find 1 and Find 2 tabs, you can compare the results of both searches.

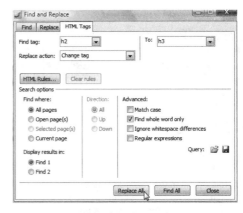

Figure 4.64 Since the action cannot be reversed, make sure you're ready before clicking Replace All.

Figure 4.65 Assuming you've doubled-checked your work, click Yes.

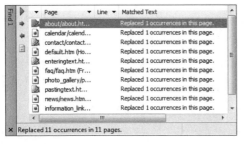

Figure 4.66 Expression Web makes the replacements and lists the actions in the Find pane.

Figure 4.67 To check the spelling of the selected page(s), choose Tools > Spelling > Spelling (top) or click the Spelling button in the Standard toolbar (bottom).

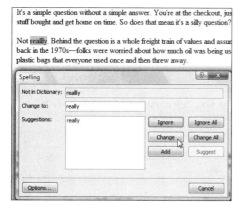

Figure 4.68 Possible misspellings are highlighted in the page while the Spelling dialog box offers suggestions.

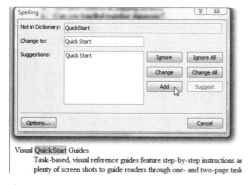

Figure 4.69 If you know the word's spelled correctly—perhaps it's a trademark—you can add it to the dictionary.

Using Spell Check, Thesaurus

Expression Web lets you check the spelling on a single page or across an entire Web site. You also can customize the spelling dictionary by adding words of your own. Finally, the built-in thesaurus can be handy when you're hunting for just the right word.

To check spelling on a single page:

1. Open the page in which you want to check the spelling. Choose Tools > Spelling > Spelling (F7), or click the Spelling button if the Standard toolbar is visible (**Figure 4.67**).

2. Expression Web highlights a possible misspelling in the page while the Spelling dialog box offers suggestions. If you want to use a suggested word, click Change or Change All if you want to fix every instance of the word on that page (**Figure 4.68**).

3. If you know the word's spelled correctly—perhaps it's a trademark that Expression Web doesn't recognize—click Ignore or Ignore All. You also can add terms to the dictionary by clicking Add (**Figure 4.69**).

4. Once the spell check is done, click OK to close the dialog box (**Figure 4.70**).

Figure 4.70 Once the spell check is done, click OK to close the dialog box.

To check spelling on multiple pages:

1. In the Folder List select the entire site or multiple pages (using Ctrl-click) in which you want to check the spelling. Choose Tools > Spelling > Spelling (F7), or click the Spelling button if the Standard toolbar is visible.

2. An alert dialog box asks you to confirm whether you want to search multiple pages or the whole site (**Figure 4.71**). Click Start to close the dialog box and begin the spell check.

3. When Expression Web displays the results, look through the Misspelled words column to quickly see what's been spotted (**Figure 4.72**).

4. Double-click a page to see the possible misspellings in context. If you want to use a suggested word, click Change or Change All if you want to fix every instance of the word on that page.

5. Once you've checked a page, Expression Web asks if you want to see the next page with misspellings (top, **Figure 4.73**). Once you've checked all the pages, Expression Web offers you to return you to the original list of pages and words (bottom, **Figure 4.73**).

6. After returning to the list of pages, Expression Web displays which pages have been fixed (Edited) and which have not (**Figure 4.74**). If you're done checking all the pages, close the Spelling dialog box by clicking the X in the upper-right corner.

Figure 4.71 An alert dialog box asks you to confirm if you want to search multiple pages or the whole site before you click Start.

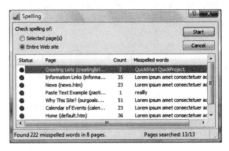

Figure 4.72 Look through the Misspelled words column to quickly see what's been spotted.

Figure 4.73 After checking a page, you can go to the next page (top). Once you've checked all the pages, you can return to the original list (bottom).

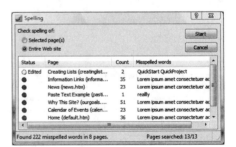

Figure 4.74 As you spell-check the listed pages, Expression Web notes which have been fixed (Edited) and which have not.

Figure 4.75 To change your spelling options, choose Tools > Spelling > Spelling Options.

Figure 4.76 To switch dictionaries or use one you've customized, click Custom Dictionaries.

Figure 4.77 To add or correct words for the default dictionary, click Edit Word List. To switch to a new *blank* dictionary, choose New or click Add to navigate to a supplemental or customized dictionary.

To change your spelling options:

1. Choose Tools > Spelling > Spelling Options (**Figure 4.75**).

2. Look through the Spelling Options dialog box's choices and select those you want to use, including Check spelling as you type (**Figure 4.76**). To switch dictionaries or use one you've customized, click Custom Dictionaries.

3. In the Custom Dictionaries dialog box, the default dictionary is highlighted (**Figure 4.77**). To add or correct words for this dictionary, click Edit Word List. To switch to a new *blank* dictionary, choose New. Click Add to navigate to a supplemental or customized dictionary of your own.

4. Choose OK to close the dialog box and apply the dictionary changes.

To use the thesaurus:

1. In any open page, select a word and choose Tools > Thesaurus (Shift F7) (**Figure 4.78**).

2. The Thesaurus dialog box lists the word on the left with its various meanings (**Figure 4.79**). Select the correct meaning at the bottom left, and then click any synonym listed on the right. Choose Look Up if you're not sure what the synonym means, or choose Replace and the selected synonym replaces the original word.

3. To close the dialog box, click Cancel or the X in the upper-right corner.

Figure 4.78 In any open page, select a word and choose Tools > Thesaurus.

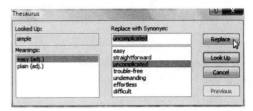

Figure 4.79 The selected word's various meanings appear at the bottom left. Pick one, and then click any synonym listed on the right and choose Replace, or Look Up if you're not sure what the synonym means.

Working with Images

While headings and text establish the underlying order for your pages, it's the images that give them interest and pizzazz. The first section of this chapter shows how to add and position images. The second section explains how to use Expression Web's built-in Pictures toolbar to adjust their appearance. To add hyperlinked hotspots within images, see "Creating an Image Hotspot" on page 117.

Adding Images

Whether it's click-and-dragging an image right into a page, navigating through your computer's files, or pulling something directly from a digital camera, Expression Web makes quick work of adding images to your pages.

To add an image:

1. Open a Web page, and click where you want to insert an image. Choose Insert > Picture, and make a source choice from the drop-down menu (**Figure 5.1**).

2. Navigate to the image you want to use, and click Insert (**Figure 5.2**).

3. Add a brief description of the image in the Alternate text box and, if you like, a more detailed one in the Long description box (**Figure 5.3**).

4. Click OK, and the image appears in the page. If necessary, press ⏎Enter to add a line break and bump the heading or text to the next line (**Figure 5.4**).

5. Save the change (Ctrl S), and if you're adding an image not already included among your Web site files, the Save Embedded Files dialog box appears (**Figure 5.5**). Click Change Folder to navigate to where on the site you want to save the image (see the sixth tip).

   When you're done click OK, and the image is saved to your chosen folder.

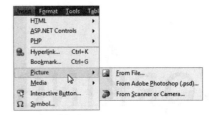

Figure 5.1 To add an image, choose Insert > Picture, and pick a source.

Figure 5.2 Navigate to the image you want to use, and click Insert.

Figure 5.3 Add a brief description in the Alternate text box, and, if you like, a more detailed one as well.

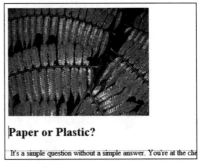

Figure 5.4 When the image appears in the page, if necessary, add a line break to bump the text to the next line.

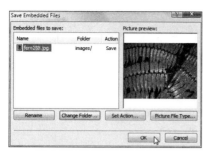

Figure 5.5 The Save Embedded Files dialog box appears whenever you save new files to your site.

Figure 5.6 The Insert Picture from File button is found in the Pictures, Standard, and Common toolbars.

Figure 5.7 Any image already in your site files can be clicked and dragged from the Folder List pane onto the page.

Figure 5.8 When navigating among files, you may find it easier to spot an image by switching your folder view to Large or Extra Large Icons.

✔ Tips

■ In step 1, if you have a digital camera or scanner connected to your computer, you can insert a picture directly from either device. But in practice, such images will be much larger than you'll want to use in a page. You're better off importing those images onto your hard drive and editing them for size *before* inserting them into your pages.

■ You also can use the Insert Picture from File button found in the Pictures, Standard, and Common toolbars (**Figure 5.6**). The Pictures toolbar includes the most used image tools, so you may want to turn it on: Choose View > Toolbars > Pictures.

■ If the image has already been saved to your site, you can click and drag it from the Folder List pane onto the page (**Figure 5.7**).

■ In step 2, you may find it easier to identify the images you want if you switch your folder view to Large or Extra Large Icons (**Figure 5.8**).

■ In step 3, the alternate text applied to an image can be read aloud by special programs used by the visually impaired. It also helps visitors with slow connections get some sense of a page's images before they finish downloading, since the text appears instantly.

■ In step 5, keep your site files tidy by saving pictures to the main images folder or—if you're dealing with hundreds of images—create a separate images folder for each section of the site.

■ The image used in this example was sized ahead of time for the space. For more information, see "Resizing and Resampling Images" on page 95.

ADDING IMAGES

To move an image:

1. Click a picture to select it, and a series of small, square handles appear on its corners and sides (**Figure 5.9**).

2. While still pressing your mouse button, drag the cursor to where you want to move the picture (**Figure 5.10**).

3. Release the cursor, and the picture moves to the new spot (**Figure 5.11**). Depending on how your text and headings flow around the picture, you may need to change the picture's wrapping style. (See "To set horizontal alignment" on the next page.)

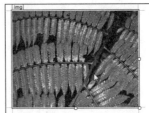

Figure 5.9 Select a picture, and clickable square handles appear on its corners and sides.

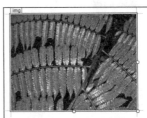

Figure 5.10 While still pressing your mouse button, drag the cursor to where you want to move the picture.

Figure 5.11 Release the cursor, and the picture moves to the new spot.

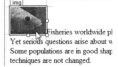

Figure 5.12 To set horizontal alignment, double-click a picture.

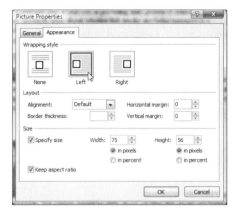

Figure 5.13 Depending on how you want text to wrap around the picture, select Left or Right in the Picture Properties dialog box.

Figure 5.14 The text and picture adjust as specified (left in this example).

Aligning Images

Horizontal alignment, sometimes called wrapping, controls how your pictures align with items to the left or right. Vertical alignment, often just called alignment, controls whether a picture sits at the same level, above, or below the items on either side of it. Those items can be pictures or text.

To set horizontal alignment (wrapping style):

1. Double-click a picture (**Figure 5.12**).

2. When the Picture Properties dialog box appears, select the Appearance tab. By default, the Wrapping style is set to None with no margins. Depending on how you want text to wrap around the picture, select Left or Right (**Figure 5.13**).

3. You also can set the picture's (vertical) alignment with the Alignment drop-down menu. (For details, see "To set vertical alignment" on the next page.)

4. Click OK to chose the dialog box and apply your changes.

    The text and picture readjust as specified (**Figure 5.14**).

✔ Tips

- If the Common or Formatting toolbar is visible, you can click the alignment buttons to set the image's wrapping style (but not its vertical alignment).

- You also can open the Picture Properties dialog box by right-clicking a picture and choosing Picture Properties in the drop-down menu.

- While the Picture Properties dialog box includes boxes for setting margins, the click-and-drag methods explained on page 88 are much easier to use.

ALIGNING IMAGES

To set vertical alignment:

1. Double-click a picture, and when the Picture Properties dialog box appears, select the Appearance tab.

   Naturally enough, the Alignment drop-down menu is normally set to Default (**Figure 5.15**).

2. Use the drop-down menu to make a choice (**Figure 5.16**). Stick to using Default, Top, Middle, and Bottom. The other alignment choices are no longer supported by modern Web browsers.

3. Click OK to chose the dialog box and apply your changes.

   The picture's alignment with the adjacent text readjusts based on your choice (**Figure 5.17**).

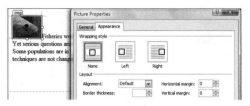

Figure 5.15 Naturally enough, the vertical alignment drop-down menu is normally set to Default.

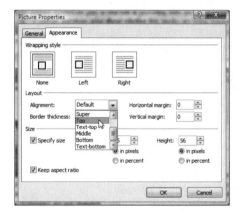

Figure 5.16 Use the drop-down menu to make a choice. Stick to using Default, Top, Middle, and Bottom.

Figure 5.17 The picture's vertical alignment with the adjacent text readjusts based on your choice (top in this example).

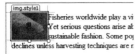

Figure 5.18 Here a left wrap has been added to the top alignment example of Figure 5.17.

Figure 5.19 Three images with the default vertical alignment.

Figure 5.20 Three images with a top vertical alignment.

Figure 5.21 The left and right images have a top alignment; the middle image has a middle alignment.

✔ Tips

■ The effect of your alignment choice depends on the selected Wrapping style. For example, compare **Figure 5.17,** which has a top alignment with no wrap, to **Figure 5.18,** which also has a top alignment but a left wrap.

■ Take a look at **Figures 5.19, 5.20,** and **5.21,** to get a sense of how the alignment choices differ.

Adding Borders, Margins, or Padding

If you find it hard sometimes to remember what's a border versus a margin or padding, take a look at **Figure 5.22.** It appears in the Box category section of the New Style dialog box and offers a quick visual primer on keeping them straight. To make things even easier, you can simply click and drag to change margins and padding. While you can adjust them for each picture, consider using CSS to create several margin/padding styles, which then can be applied to pictures across the site. For more information, see "Creating Styles with CSS" on page 123.

To add borders to an image:

1. In Design or Split view, click the picture to which you want to add a border (**Figure 5.23**).

2. Choose Format > Borders and Shading (**Figure 5.24**).

   In the Borders and Shading dialog box, the Borders tab is selected by default (**Figure 5.25**).

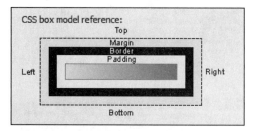

Figure 5.22 A handy graphic from the New Style dialog box shows the differences between borders, margins, and padding.

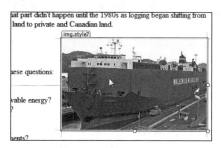

Figure 5.23 Select the image to which you want to apply a border.

Figure 5.24 Choose Format > Borders and Shading to reach the Borders and Shading dialog box.

Figure 5.25 The Borders tab is selected by default.

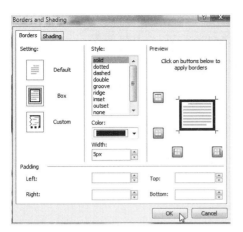

Figure 5.26 Make your Setting, Style, Color, and Width choices based on what you see in the Preview area.

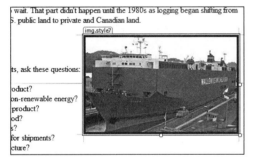

Figure 5.27 The border choices made in step 3 applied to the image.

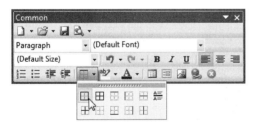

Figure 5.28 You can quickly add a 1-pixel-wide black border to an image by clicking the Picture toolbar's Border button and selecting the first button in the drop-down menu.

3. Make your Setting, Style, Color, and Width choices based on what you see in the Preview area (**Figure 5.26**). Click OK. The dialog box closes, and the border is applied (**Figure 5.27**).

✔ Tips

- If you want to change the border, choose Format > Borders and Shading again and make new choices in the Borders and Shading dialog box.

- In the Borders and Shading dialog box, select Default to immediately remove the border entirely. If you just press (Backspace) to make the text box blank, the border will not disappear.

- If the Common toolbar is turned on, you can quickly add a 1-pixel-wide black border around the entire image by clicking the Border button and selecting the first button in the drop-down menu (**Figure 5.28**).

ADDING BORDERS TO AN IMAGE

To add margins to an image:

1. In Design or Split view, click the picture, and at its corners you see thin, beige lines. Move your cursor over any line, and the cursor becomes a two-headed arrow (**Figure 5.29**).

2. Click and drag the line to change the horizontal margin, using the small margin size box as a guide (**Figure 5.30**). Release the cursor when you're satisfied with the size.

3. Use the same method to adjust the vertical margin if needed (**Figure 5.31**). Release the cursor when you're satisfied (**Figure 5.32**).

4. Be sure to save your changes ((Ctrl)(S)).

✔ Tips

- In step 1, if you see a *four*-headed arrow, you need to move the cursor out from the edge of the image until it becomes a *two*-headed arrow.

- Small diagonal lines fill the image's margin area, giving you another way to gauge its size.

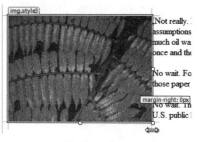

Figure 5.29 To add margins to an image, click and drag the thin beige lines appearing at the corners.

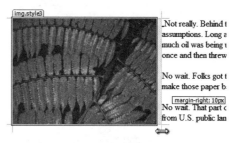

Figure 5.30 Click and drag the line to change the horizontal margin, using the small margin size box as a guide.

Figure 5.31 You can use the same method to adjust the vertical margin.

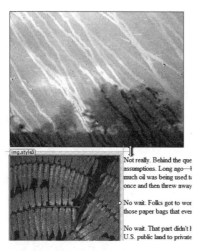

Figure 5.32 Release the cursor when you've adjusted the margins to your satisfaction.

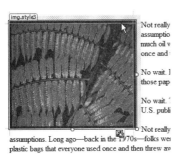

assumptions. Long ago—back in the 1970s—folks were plastic bags that everyone used once and then threw aw

Figure 5.33 Click on the picture and press [Shift], and four, light-blue lines appear *inside* the picture's edge.

assumptions. Long ago—back in the 1970s—plastic bags that everyone used once and then

Figure 5.34 Click and drag any of the lines to add padding to that side of the picture, using the small padding size box as a guide.

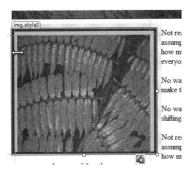

Figure 5.35 You can add padding to any side of the image.

To add padding to an image:

1. In Design or Split view, click on the picture and press [Shift], and four, light-blue lines appear *inside* the picture's edge (**Figure 5.33**).

2. Click and drag any of the lines to add padding to that side of the picture, using the small padding size box as a guide (**Figure 5.34**). Release the cursor when you're satisfied with the amount of padding.

3. If you want to add padding to any side of the picture, repeat step 2 (**Figure 5.35**).

4. Be sure to save your changes ([Ctrl][S]).

✔ Tips

- The light-blue padding lines actually extend beyond the picture's edge but are harder to see there, especially against a white page background.

- If you have a hard time distinguishing the light-blue padding lines from the light-beige margin lines, select the picture and press [Shift] two or three times. Expression Web toggles between highlighting the padding and margin lines.

ADDING PADDING TO AN IMAGE

Editing Images

For major image editing, it's best to use a dedicated graphics program, but the Pictures toolbar can handle lots of simple editing tasks. Whether you want to flip an image, adjust its contrast, or make it black and white, the basic steps remain the same. See "To make simple image changes" on the next page. The rest of the chapter explains more involved tasks: cropping, resizing or resampling, making thumbnails, and setting a transparent color.

When you edit an image, you have the option of saving the changes as a new file or replacing the original. To be extra safe, always keep a duplicate of the original image stored outside your Web site. The Restore button, explained first because it lets you undo edits, quickly becomes one of your best safeguards against mistakes.

Figure 5.36 To make simple editing changes, begin by selecting the image.

Figure 5.37 Click the appropriate button in the Pictures toolbar (in this case, the horizontal flip button).

Figure 5.38 The image in the Web page changes based on your choice.

To make simple image changes:

1. In Design or Split view, click the picture you want to change (**Figure 5.36**).

2. Click the appropriate button in the Pictures toolbar (**Figure 5.37**). (See "Picture Toolbar Options" below.)

   The image in the Web page changes based on your choice (**Figure 5.38**).

3. To save your changes, see "To save image changes" on the next page.

To restore an edited image:

1. If after making an edit, you want to undo the change, click the Restore button 🖫.

   The image reverts to its appearance before the most recent change.

2. Continue clicking the Restore button to step backward through the changes made since the last time the image was saved.

✔ Tip

■ The Restore button only works if you have not saved the changes.

EDITING IMAGES

Table 5.1

Pictures Toolbar Options	
Use	**To**
🖼	Insert a picture from your computer, digital camera, or scanner
🖼	Create smaller version of image linked to larger original (See "To create a thumbnail image" on page 97.)
🖼 or 🖼	Rotate picture to left or right
🖼 or ◀	Flip picture horizontally or vertically
◑↑ or ◑↓	Increase or decrease picture's contrast
☀↑ or ☀↓	Increase or decrease picture's brightness
⊹	Crop picture (See "To crop an image" on page 94.)
✏	Make one color in the picture transparent (See "To set transparency" on page 103.)
⬛⬛	Make a picture black and white or wash out the color
🖼	Add a bevel around a picture
🖼	Resample a picture (See "Resizing and Resampling Images" on page 95.)
▢ ◯ ⬔ 🖫	Create hyperlinked hotspots in picture (See "To create hotspots" on page 117.)
🖫	Restore image to its appearance before changes

To save image changes:

1. To save any changes you make to a picture, press ⎡Ctrl⎤⎡S⎤. In the Save Embedded Files dialog box, which lists all the files you've changed, select an image to save (**Figure 5.39**).

2. If you want to save the edited version as a *new file,* click Rename and type a new name (leave the suffix .jpg as is) (**Figure 5.40**). The pending Action listed for the file changes from Overwrite to Save (**Figure 5.41**). Click OK.

   or

   If you want to *replace* the original image file with your changes, simply click OK.

3. Based on your choice in step 2, the edited picture replaces the original or is saved as a new file.

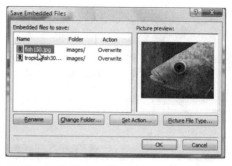

Figure 5.39 The Save Embedded Files dialog box lists all the files you've changed or added since your last sitewide save.

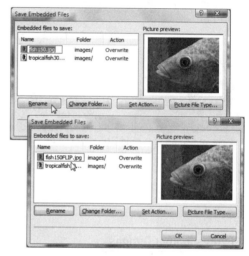

Figure 5.40 To save the edited version as a *new file,* click Rename and type a new name (leave the suffix .jpg as is).

Figure 5.41 Once you rename the file, the pending Action changes from Overwrite to Save.

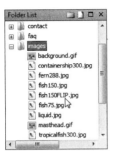

Figure 5.42 When you rename an edited image, a new file is added to the Folder List.

✔ Tips

■ If you rename the edited image, that new file is added to the Folder List (**Figure 5.42**).

■ Web sites often contain hundreds of images, especially since you often need multiple sizes of the same image for different sections of your layouts. For that reason, naming an image `treefern_small.jpg`, as Expression Web does, isn't specific enough. If my site's page layouts typically need images 50, 100, and 288 pixels wide, I name the images accordingly: `treefern50.jpg`, `treefern100.jpg`, and `treefern288.jpg`. I instantly know which version to grab when navigating through file lists, and by putting the number at the end of the name, all those tree images are listed together. When I need to generate a new image size, this same scheme makes it obvious that the original file is named `treefern`.

SAVING IMAGE CHANGES

To crop an image:

1. In Design or Split view, click the picture that you want to crop (**Figure 5.43**).

2. Click the Crop button in the Pictures toolbar (**Figure 5.44**).

3. A dashed line appears in the picture, marking the crop boundaries (**Figure 5.45**). Click and drag any of the small, square handles to resize and reposition the crop boundaries (**Figure 5.46**).

4. Click the Crop button again, or double-click any of the handles, or press ↵Enter. The picture is cropped to the boundaries (**Figure 5.47**).

5. Save your changes (Ctrl S), as explained in "To save image changes" on page 92.

Figure 5.43
Click to select the picture you want to crop.

Figure 5.44 Click the Crop button in the Pictures toolbar.

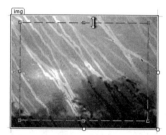

Figure 5.45
A dashed line appears in the picture, marking the crop boundaries.

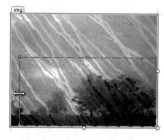

Figure 5.46
Click and drag any of the small, square handles to resize and reposition the crop boundaries.

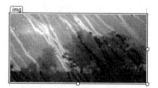

Figure 5.47 Click the Crop button again, double-click any of the handles, or press ↵Enter, and the crop is applied.

Figure 5.48 To quickly resize an image, click any of the square handles along the edge.

Figure 5.49 Click and drag to resize the image on the fly.

Figure 5.50 Release the cursor, and the image assumes its new size.

Figure 5.51 To resample the resized image, click the Resample button in the Pictures toolbar.

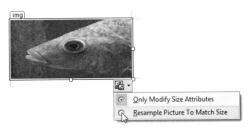

Figure 5.52 You also can click the button at the image's lower right and choose Resample Picture To Match Size.

Resizing and Resampling Images

Whenever you insert an image on a page, its dimensions are automatically included in the HTML coding. If you want to significantly *enlarge* an image, you'll get better looking results going back to the original image and using a dedicated graphics program to create a new version for importing to the site. However, if you only need to make relatively minor size adjustments (10 percent or less), you can just resize and resample the original. Another way to deal with larger images is to create a series of quick-to-download thumbnail images that link to larger, higher quality versions.

To manually resize and resample an image:

1. In Design or Split view, click the picture and then drag any of the square-shaped along its edge to a new position (**Figures 5.48** and **5.49**). A tooltip displays the new dimensions as you drag.

2. Release the cursor.

   The image assumes its new size (**Figure 5.50**).

3. To resample the resized image, click the Resample button in the Pictures toolbar (**Figure 5.51**). You also can click the Picture Actions button at the image's lower right and choose Resample Picture To Match Size (**Figure 5.52**).

   The picture is resampled, though you may not see a significant difference.

4. Save your changes ([Ctrl][S]) as explained in "To save image changes" on page 92.

RESIZING AND RESAMPLING IMAGES

To precisely resize and resample an image:

1. In Design or Split view, double-click a picture. When the Picture Properties dialog box appears, select the Appearance tab.

2. Select the Specify size checkbox, and in the Width or Height text box type the size (pixels or percent) you want (top, **Figure 5.53**). If you also select Keep aspect ratio, the number in the other dimension text box automatically changes in response to your entry to maintain the image's proportions (bottom, **Figure 5.53**). Click OK.

The dialog box closes, and the image changes to match the new dimensions.

3. To resample the image, click the Resample button in the Pictures toolbar. You also can click the Picture Actions button at the image's lower right and choose Resample Picture To Match Size.

The picture is resampled to match the new size.

4. Save your changes (Ctrl S), as explained in "To save image changes" on page 92.

✔ Tip

■ In step 2, if you uncheck the Keep aspect ratio checkbox, you can size the width and height independently (**Figure 5.54**).

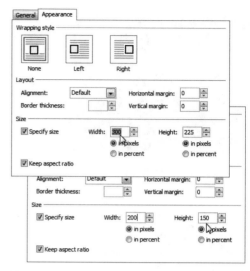

Figure 5.53 To precisely resize an image, select the Specify size checkbox and use the Width or Height text boxes (top). If you select Keep aspect ratio, the number in the other dimension text box automatically changes in response to your entry to maintain the proportions (bottom).

Figure 5.54 If you uncheck the Keep aspect ratio checkbox, you can size the width and height independently.

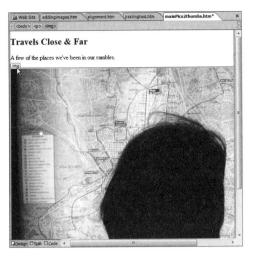

Figure 5.55 Insert and then select the large version of the image for which you want to create a thumbnail.

Figure 5.56 In the Pictures toolbar, click the Auto Thumbnail button (Ctrl T).

Figure 5.57 The large, original image is replaced by a thumbnail image.

To create a thumbnail image:

1. In Design or Split view, insert the large version of the image for which you want to create a thumbnail and then click to select the image (**Figure 5.55**).

2. In the Pictures toolbar, click the Auto Thumbnail button (Ctrl T) (**Figure 5.56**). The original image is replaced by a thumbnail image (**Figure 5.57**).

3. Continue to add large, original images to the page as needed, repeating step 2 with each one (**Figure 5.58**).

4. Save your changes (Ctrl S), as explained in "To save image changes" on page 92.

(continued)

Figure 5.58 Continue adding large images to the page and converting them to thumbnails as needed.

CREATING THUMBNAILS

5. To view the page of thumbnails in your Web browser, press F12.

Your default Web browser launches and displays the page of thumbnails (**Figure 5.59**).

6. Click any thumbnail in your Web browser, and the larger, original image is displayed (**Figure 5.60**).

✔ Tips

- You don't need to create a page beforehand to hold the larger image. Using these steps, any image file in your Folder List is served up to the browser from the automatically linked thumbnail.

- In step 2, you also can right-click the large image and choose Auto Thumbnail in the drop-down menu (**Figure 5.61**).

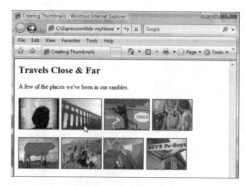

Figure 5.59 To view the thumbnails page in your Web browser, press F12 and click any image.

Figure 5.60 Your browser immediately retrieves and displays the large, original image.

Figure 5.61 You also can right-click the large image and choose Auto Thumbnail in the drop-down menu.

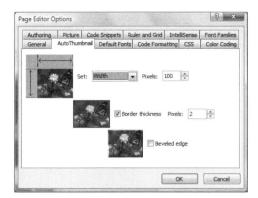

Figure 5.62 To see the default settings, select the Auto Thumbnail tab in the Page Editor Options dialog box.

Figure 5.63 Use the Set drop-down menu to change which aspect of the thumbnail's size to control.

To change the thumbnail default size:

1. Choose Tools > Page Editor Options. Select the Auto Thumbnail tab to see the default settings (**Figure 5.62**).

2. Use the Set drop-down menu to change which aspect of the thumbnail's size to control (**Figure 5.63**). Type a number in the Pixels box. If you want a border applied, leave Border thickness selected and type how many pixels wide it should be. You also can add a beveled edge.

3. Click OK to close the dialog box and apply the settings to future thumbnails.

Setting Image Formats

Just two file formats are used for virtually all Web images: GIFs and JPEGs. GIFs (CompuServe's Graphics Interchange Format) work best for buttons, solid blocks of color, and illustrations. JPEGs (originally developed by the Joint Photographic Experts Group) work best for photos since they can display millions of colors in relatively compact files. A third file format, PNG (Portable Network Graphics) is slowly gaining acceptance now that version 4 and later Web browsers support the format. PNG files compress images nicely without losing as much information as a JPEG and sidestep an ongoing legal dispute over GIF rights.

By default, Expression Web saves photos as JPEGs, with a quality level of 90, which is fairly high. If you really need to shave some bits off photo files, you could change them to the PNG format or lower their default JPEG quality to around 60 to 65, which still mostly avoids adding jagged lines to the image. For more information, see "To change image format defaults" on the next page. You also have the option of changing those settings for a single image. For more information, see "To change a single image's format" on page 102.

When using GIFs for buttons, it can be handy to set a single color as transparent. That enables you, for example, to create the illusion of a round or irregularly shaped button by setting the color to match the page's background color. For more information, see "To set transparency" on page 103.

Figure 5.64 To change image format defaults, click the File Type Settings button in the Pictures tab of the Page Editor Options dialog box.

Figure 5.65 Use the checkboxes to change the GIF defaults and the text boxes to change the JPEG defaults.

Figure 5.66 Click OK to close the dialog box, and the settings are applied to any newly created images.

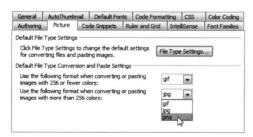

Figure 5.67 To save all your photos as PNG files instead of JPEGs, select png in the second drop-down menu.

To change image format defaults:

1. Choose Tools > Page Editor Options > Picture, and click the File Type Settings button (**Figure 5.64**).

2. In the Picture File Type dialog box, use the checkboxes to change your GIF default and the text boxes for your JPEG defaults (**Figure 5.65**).

3. Click OK to close the dialog box and apply the settings to newly created images (**Figure 5.66**).

✔ Tips

- In step 1, if you want to save all your photos as PNG files instead of JPEGs, select png in the second drop-down menu (**Figure 5.67**).

- In step 2, unless you'll be creating lots of GIF buttons with transparent edges to show the background color, it's best not to select Transparent, since you can set this feature individually in your images (**Figure 5.65**).

SETTING IMAGE FORMATS

To change a single image's format:

1. Double-click an image on a Web page to open the Picture Properties dialog box.

2. Select the Appearance tab, and click Picture File Type (**Figure 5.68**).

3. Select another format (**Figure 5.69**). You also can change the quality level for a JPEG file by unchecking the Use image as is checkbox and then entering new settings in the Quality and Progressive passes text boxes.

4. Click OK to close the dialog box and apply the settings to the selected image (**Figure 5.70**). When the Picture Properties dialog box reappears, click OK to close it.

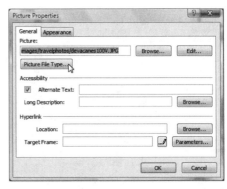

Figure 5.68 To change a single image's format, click Picture File Type in the Appearance tab.

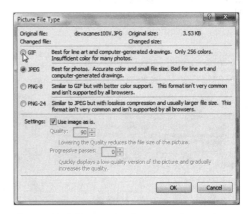

Figure 5.69 Select another format, or change the quality level for a JPEG file by clearing the Use image as is checkbox.

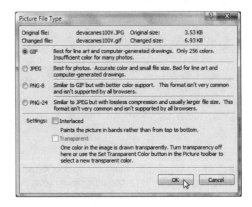

Figure 5.70 Click OK to close the dialog box and apply the settings to the selected image.

Figure 5.71 Select the picture to which you want to apply transparency to match the page background.

Figure 5.72 Click the Set Transparent Color button in the Pictures toolbar.

Figure 5.73 If the selected image is formatted as a JPEG, an alert dialog box offers to convert the image to a GIF.

Figure 5.74 Click the eraser on the color you want to become transparent.

Figure 5.75 The targeted color becomes transparent, allowing the page's background color to show through.

To set transparency:

1. In Design or Split view, click to select the picture to which you want to apply transparency (**Figure 5.71**).

2. Click the Set Transparent Color button in the Pictures toolbar (**Figure 5.72**).

3. If the selected image is formatted as a JPEG, which doesn't support transparency, click OK when an alert dialog box offers to convert the image to the GIF format (**Figure 5.73**).

4. As you move the cursor arrow over the selected image, it becomes a pencil eraser (**Figure 5.74**). Click the eraser on the color you want to become transparent.

   The targeted color becomes transparent, allowing the page's background color to show through (**Figure 5.75**).

CREATING LINKS

The Web's power springs from the user's ability to jump from file to file anywhere in the world. Hyperlinks make that possible. Hyperlinks, or simply links, come in several varieties: external links to anywhere in the world, links to other spots in the same document, links to send email, and links embedded in pictures. Expression Web makes it easy to create them all. Changing the default link colors, by the way, is covered in "Creating Styles with CSS" on page 123.

Adding Links

Some of your links will point to a file out on the Web. Many of your links will point to another page within your Web site. Expression Web automatically creates *absolute* links to those external Web files and a *relative* links to pages in your Web site. Absolute links always include the full URL, including the http protocol: `http://www.waywest.net/expression/`. Relative links include just the file name and enclosing folder: `/ExamplePages/creatinglinks.htm`. The great advantage of relative links is that you can rearrange your site as much as you like, and Expression Web keeps all your links intact.

To link to a page in your Web site:

1. Select the text you want to link, right-click, and choose Hyperlink from the drop-down menu (**Figure 6.1**).

2. By default, the Insert Hyperlink dialog box shows your current site (**Figure 6.2**). Use the center area to navigate to the target of your link, and once it's selected, click OK (**Figure 6.3**).

   The dialog box closes, and the selected text is linked to the other page (**Figure 6.4**).

✔ Tip

- In step 1, you also can select the text and click the Hyperlink button in the Standard toolbar (**Figure 6.5**).

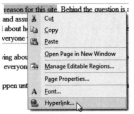

Figure 6.1 Select the text you want to link, right-click, and choose Hyperlink.

Figure 6.2 By default, the Insert Hyperlink dialog box shows your current site.

Figure 6.3 Use the center area to navigate to the target of your link, and once it's selected, click OK.

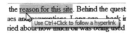

Figure 6.4 The selected text is linked to the other page.

Figure 6.5 You also can select the text and click the Hyperlink button in the Standard toolbar.

Figure 6.6 To link to a not-yet-created page, click the Create New Document button (top). Name the new page, and select Edit the new document later (bottom).

To link to a not-yet-created page:

1. Select the text you want to link, right-click, and choose Hyperlink from the drop-down menu.

2. Click the Create New Document button in the Insert Hyperlink dialog box (top, **Figure 6.6**). Name the new page, and if you don't want to stop what you're doing, select Edit the new document later (bottom, **Figure 6.6**).

3. Click OK.

   The dialog box closes, and the new blank page is created and added to the Folder List.

To link to an external Web page:

1. Select the text you want to link, right-click, and choose Hyperlink from the drop-down menu.

2. Click the Browse the Web button (**Figure 6.7**).

   If it is not already running, your default Web browser launches.

3. Surf to the page to which you want to link, and press Alt Tab.

   The Insert Hyperlink dialog box reappears with the page's address inserted in the Address text box (**Figure 6.8**).

4. Click OK.

   The dialog box closes, and the selected text is linked to the external Web address (**Figure 6.9**).

✔ Tips

- In step 2, if you know the Web address, you can type directly in the Address text box.

- In step 3, you also can use the Address drop-down menu to select recently visited Web pages (**Figure 6.10**).

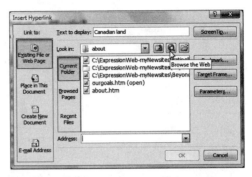

Figure 6.7 To link to an external Web page, click the Browse the Web button.

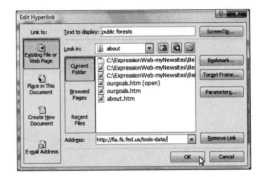

Figure 6.8 After finding the page with your Web browser, press *at* and its address appears in the Address text box.

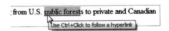

Figure 6.9 The selected text now is linked to the external Web address.

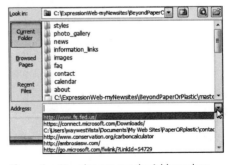

Figure 6.10 You also can use the Address drop-down menu to select recently visited Web pages.

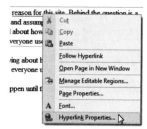

Figure 6.11 To change a link, right-click and choose Hyperlink Properties.

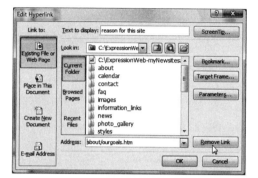

Figure 6.12 To remove a link, click Remove Link in the Edit Hyperlink dialog box.

To change a link:

1. Right-click the linked text, and choose Hyperlink Properties from the drop-down menu (**Figure 6.11**).

2. In the Edit Hyperlink dialog box, surf to a new site, navigate to another page, or use the Address drop-down menu to make a new choice.

3. Click OK.

   The dialog box closes, and the selected text is linked to your new address choice.

To remove a link:

1. Right-click the linked text. and choose Hyperlink from the drop-down menu.

2. In the Edit Hyperlink dialog box, click Remove Link (**Figure 6.12**).

   The dialog box closes, and the selected text is no longer linked.

CHANGING, REMOVING LINKS

To create an email link:

1. Right-click the linked text, and choose Hyperlink from the drop-down menu.

2. In the Insert Hyperlink dialog box, click E-mail Address (**Figure 6.13**).

3. Type a subject and an address; Expression Web automatically includes mailto: at the beginning (**Figure 6.14**).

4. Click OK.

   The dialog box closes, and the selected text is linked to the new email address.

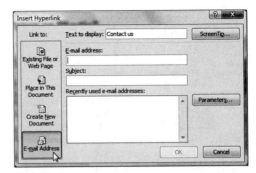

Figure 6.13 To create an email link, click E-mail Address in the Edit Hyperlink dialog box.

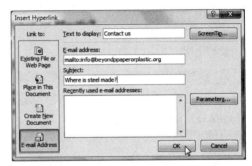

Figure 6.14 Type a subject and an address; Expression Web automatically includes mailto:.

Figure 6.15 To set a link target, click Target Frame in the Edit Hyperlink dialog box.

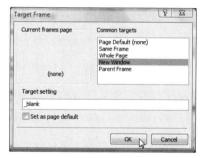

Figure 6.16 Select New Window in the Target Frame dialog box.

Targeting Links

Normally when you click a hyperlink, your Web browser replaces the current page with the new page. You can, however, set the link so that the new (target) page opens in a new window. This can be useful for external links, since your visitor can still see your site in the original window.

To set a link target:

1. Right-click an existing text link, and choose Hyperlink from the drop-down menu.

2. In the Edit Hyperlink dialog box, click Target Frame (**Figure 6.15**).

3. In the Target Frame dialog box, select New Window (**Figure 6.16**).

4. Click OK.

   The dialog box closes, and the Edit Hyperlink dialog box reappears.

5. Click OK.

   The Edit Hyperlink dialog box closes, and the change is applied to the linked text.

✔ Tips

- If your site uses frames, you also can choose Same Frame or Parent Frame. But many search engines have trouble reading frames, so consider switching your site to CSS positioning in the long run.

- In step 3, if you want all your links to open in a new window, select Set as page default.

TARGETING LINKS

Adding ScreenTips

Expression Web calls them ScreenTips, JavaScript call them tooltips; but whatever their name, they're a common sight on the Web. Roll your cursor over a link on a Web page, and a little tag appears that provides a clue about the linked content. You don't have to create them of course, but they do help visitors find their way around, so add them when you can.

To add a ScreenTip:

1. Right-click an existing text link, and choose Hyperlink from the drop-down menu.

2. In the Edit Hyperlink dialog box, click ScreenTip (**Figure 6.17**).

3. In the Set Hyperlink ScreenTip dialog box, type the tip (**Figure 6.18**).

4. Click OK.
   The dialog box closes, and the Edit Hyperlink dialog box reappears.

5. Click OK.
   The Edit Hyperlink dialog box closes, and the change is applied to the linked text.

6. Press F12 to launch your default Web browser, and roll your cursor over the text to test the ScreenTip (**Figure 6.19**).

✔ Tip

■ ScreenTips work in most modern browsers, not just Internet Explorer.

Figure 6.17 Click ScreenTip in the Edit Hyperlink dialog box.

Figure 6.18 Add the tip text, and click OK.

Figure 6.19 In a Web browser, roll your cursor over the text to test the ScreenTip.

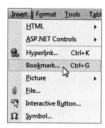

Figure 6.20 To create a book-mark, select the text and choose Insert > Bookmark.

Figure 6.21 The Bookmark dialog box automatically uses the selected text as the bookmark's name.

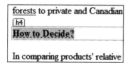

Figure 6.22 The bookmark is underlined with dashes.

Adding Bookmarks (Anchors)

Bookmarks, often called anchor links, let visitors jump to specific spots, such as section headings, in a long Web page. Creating anchors is a two-step process: first you create the bookmark itself (the anchor), and then you create the hyperlink that points to the bookmark.

To create a bookmark:

1. Select the text you want the reader to jump to, that is, the target or destination.

2. Choose Insert > Bookmark ($\boxed{\text{Ctrl}}\boxed{\text{G}}$) (**Figure 6.20**).

3. The Bookmark dialog box automatically uses the selected text as the bookmark's name (**Figure 6.21**). If you prefer, type another name.

4. Click OK.

   The dialog box closes, and the selected text is bookmarked, indicated by a dashed underline (**Figure 6.22**). See the next step to link to the bookmark.

ADDING A BOOKMARK

To link to a bookmark:

1. Select the text you linked to a bookmark, right-click, and choose Hyperlink from the drop-down menu.

2. In the Insert Hyperlink dialog box, navigate to the page containing the bookmark (anchor). Select it in the main window, and click Bookmark (**Figure 6.23**).

3. In the Select Place in Document dialog box, select the bookmark you want to use (**Figure 6.24**). In the example, there's only one, but you may have pages with multiple bookmarks from which to choose.

4. Click OK.

   The dialog box closes, and the Insert Hyperlink dialog box reappears.

5. Click OK (**Figure 6.25**).

   The Insert Hyperlink dialog box closes, and the selected text is now linked to the bookmark.

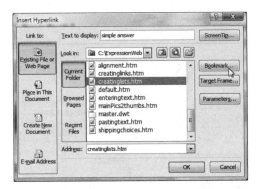

Figure 6.23 To link to a bookmark, navigate to the page and click Bookmark.

Figure 6.24 Select the bookmark, and click OK.

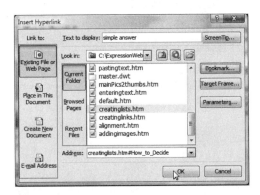

Figure 6.25 Click OK to close the dialog box and apply the link.

Figure 6.26 To clear a bookmark, right-click the text and choose Bookmark Properties.

Figure 6.27 Select the bookmark's name, and click Clear.

To clear a bookmark:

1. Select the text you previously marked as a bookmark. Right-click, and choose Bookmark Properties in the drop-down menu (**Figure 6.26**).

2. Select the bookmark's name, and click Clear (**Figure 6.27**).

3. Click OK to close the Bookmark dialog box.

   The selected text is no longer bookmarked.

Creating Image Links

You can link an entire image to a file, or you can create what's called a hotspot, which links a defined area within the image to another file. By putting multiple hotspots in an image, you can create multiple links to multiple files.

To link an entire image to a file:

1. Open the page containing the image you want linked. Right-click the image, and choose Hyperlink from the drop-down menu (**Figure 6.28**).

2. In the Insert Hyperlink dialog box, navigate to the page to which you want to link, and click OK (**Figure 6.29**).

   The dialog box closes, and the selected image is linked to the selected page.

Figure 6.28 To link an entire image to a file, right-click the image and choose Hyperlink.

Figure 6.29 Navigate to the page to which you want to link, and click OK.

Figure 6.30 To create an image hotspot, click one of the three hotspot buttons in the Pictures toolbar.

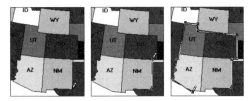

Figure 6.31 When you choose a shape, the cursor arrow becomes a pencil, allowing you to draw the hotspot's boundary.

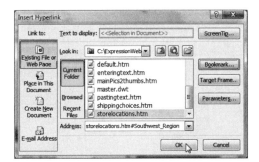

Figure 6.32 Navigate to the desired file or bookmark that you want linked to the hotspot.

To create an image hotspot:

1. Click the image in which you want to create hotspots.

2. In the Pictures toolbar, click one of the three hotspot buttons (rectangle, circle, polygon) (**Figure 6.30**).

3. When you choose a shape, the cursor arrow becomes a pencil, allowing you to draw the hotspot's boundary in the image (**Figure 6.31**). Outline the boundary, clicking whenever you need to change direction.

4. Double-click when you finish outlining boundary.

   The Insert Hyperlink dialog box appears, allowing you to navigate to the desired file or bookmark (**Figure 6.32**). (For more on using the dialog box, see "To link to a page in your Web site" on page 106.) In the example, the hotspot links to a bookmark.

5. Click OK.

   The dialog box closes, and the area is linked to the file.

6. Repeat the steps to add multiple hotspots linked to multiple files.

✔ Tips

■ Press Esc if you need to start over drawing a polygon.

■ Hotspots cannot overlap or extend beyond the image boundaries. For both reasons, you may realize that the image itself needs enlarging. Just grab one of the image's handles and drag it to give your hotspot more room, and then reposition and resize the hotspots as needed. If you wind up enlarging the image by more than 10 percent, however, go back to your original and create a fresh, larger version. Otherwise, the image winds up looking fuzzy.

To adjust a hotspot:

1. Select any handle along the hotspot's boundary (**Figure 6.33**).

2. Click and drag the handle to a new position, and then release the cursor button (**Figure 6.34**).

3. Continue adjusting the hotspot handles as necessary until you're done.

To find hotspot boundaries:

1. If you're having trouble finding hotspots within an image, select the image and click the Highlight Hotspots button in the Pictures toolbar (**Figure 6.35**).

   The image disappears, enabling you to see all the image's hotspots (**Figure 6.36**).

2. Click the Highlight Hotspots button again.

   You return to the regular view of the image, where you can then adjust the boundaries as needed.

To change or delete a hotspot link:

1. Double-click the hotspot whose link needs changing.

   The Edit Hyperlink dialog box appears.

2. Navigate to your new link target file or bookmark, or click Remove Link.

3. Click OK.

   The Edit Hyperlink dialog box closes, and the link is updated or removed.

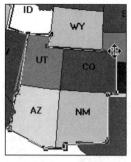

Figure 6.33 To adjust a hotspot, select any handle along the boundary.

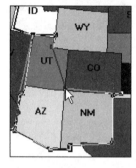

Figure 6.34 Click and drag the handle to a new position.

Figure 6.35 To find hotspot boundaries, click the Highlight Hotspots button in the Pictures toolbar.

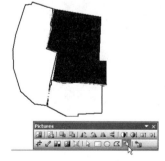

Figure 6.36 The image disappears, enabling you to see all the hotspots.

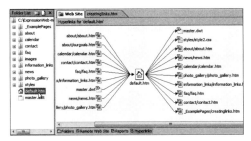

Figure 6.37 The Hyperlinks view displays every link to and from a page.

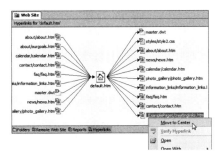

Figure 6.38 To examine a particular page, right-click the page and choose Move to Center.

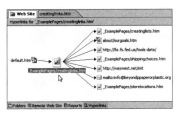

Figure 6.39 The view shifts the selected page to the center and displays its links.

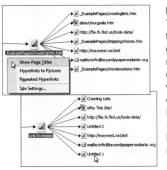

Figure 6.40
To see page titles instead of file/path names, right-click the view window and choose Show Page Titles (top). It also helps spot still-untitled pages (bottom).

Using the Hyperlinks Tools

Switching to the Hyperlinks view enables you to quickly spot, and then repair, any broken links in your Web site. Always test your links; nothing turns off visitors more than broken links.

To use the Hyperlinks view:

1. With a Web site open, click the Web Site tab at the top of the Editing window, and then click the Hyperlinks button at the bottom of the window.

2. For an overview of your site, click the home page (default.htm in our example). The Hyperlinks view displays every link to and from the home page (**Figure 6.37**).

3. To examine a particular page, right-click the page and choose Move to Center from the drop-down menu (**Figure 6.38**). The Hyperlinks view shifts the selected page to the center and displays all its links (**Figure 6.39**).

✔ Tip

■ If you'd rather see page titles instead of file/path names, right-click the view window and choose Show Page Titles in the drop-down menu (**Figure 6.40**). It also helps you spot still-untitled pages.

To check a single link:

◆ In the Hyperlinks view, right-click an external link and choose Verify Hyperlink from the drop-down menu (**Figure 6.41**).

If the link is broken, the arrow connecting the file displays a break (**Figure 6.42**). To repair any problems, see "To fix broken links" on page 122.

✔ Tip

■ You must be connected to the Internet to verify external links.

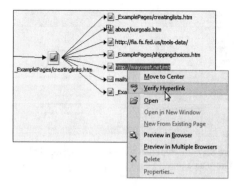

Figure 6.41 To check a single link, right-click it and choose Verify Hyperlink.

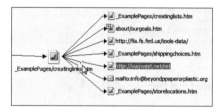

Figure 6.42 If the link is broken, the arrow connecting the file displays a break.

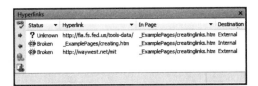

Figure 6.43 The Hyperlinks pane lists bad internal links with a broken chain and unverified external links with a question mark.

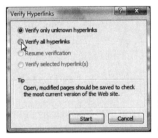

Figure 6.44 Select Verify all hyperlinks and click Start.

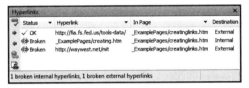

Figure 6.45 The Hyperlinks pane summarizes the status of the site's links.

To check a site's links:

1. Choose Task Panes > Hyperlinks to display the Hyperlinks pane.

   The Hyperlinks pane lists bad internal links with a broken chain and unverified external links with a question mark (**Figure 6.43**).

2. Click the Verify Hyperlink button (⬚) to start the check.

3. In the Verify Hyperlinks dialog box, go ahead and select Verify all hyperlinks (**Figure 6.44**). Click Start.

4. After a brief pause while the links are checked, the Hyperlinks pane summarizes the status of the site's links (**Figure 6.45**). To repair any problems, see "To fix broken links" on the next page.

To fix broken links:

1. In the Hyperlinks pane, right-click a broken link and choose Edit Hyperlink in the drop-down menu (**Figure 6.46**).

2. In the Edit Hyperlink dialog box, click Browse to navigate to the link's intended target page (**Figure 6.47**).

3. Once you've selected the correct page, the Edit Hyperlink dialog box reappears. Decide whether you want to fix the broken link in all pages (the default, and most likely, choice) or only selected pages (**Figure 6.48**). Click Replace.

   After taking a moment to repair the link, the Hyperlinks pane reappears and a previously broken *internal* link is removed from the list (**Figure 6.49**).

   or

   When an *external* link is repaired, the Hyperlinks pane displays a question mark and lists its status as Unknown (**Figure 6.50**). Click the Verify Hyperlink button () to run the Verify Hyperlinks dialog box again. (See "To check a site's links" on the previous page.) After verifying the link, the Hyperlinks dialog box replaces the question mark with a checkmark (**Figure 6.51**).

4. Continue working through the list until you repair all the broken links.

✔ Tip

- The bottom of the Hyperlinks pane tells you when you've fixed all the broken links (**Figure 6.51**).

Figure 6.51 After the link is verified, the question mark is replaced with a checkmark.

Figure 6.46 To fix a broken link in the Hyperlinks pane, right-click it and choose Edit Hyperlink.

Figure 6.47 Click Browse to navigate to the link's intended target page.

Figure 6.48 Once you've selected the correct page, click Replace.

Figure 6.49 The previously broken *internal* link is removed from the list.

Figure 6.50 When an *external* link is repaired, the Hyperlinks pane displays a question mark and lists its status as Unknown. Click the Verify Hyperlink button.

CREATING
STYLES WITH CSS

Why all the fuss about Cascading Style Sheets? Because, in theory, CSS lets you separate your content from its design and layout. That allows you to take the same information and reformat it for different devices, from huge computer monitors to tiny cell phones to whatever's invented next. "In theory" because untangling content and design can get confusing. Plus, unlike print design where you can exert absolute control over how things look, CSS deliberately cedes some of that control to your visitors and their various Web browsers. Striking the right balance can be tough, but Expression Web makes it easier with some of the best CSS tools found in any program.

After explaining these tools and the cascading aspect of CSS, this chapter shows you how to create two types of styles: tag-based and class-based. Tag-based styles, also known as element-based styles, apply to a specific HTML element, such as every h1 header or hyperlink. Class-based styles can be applied even if there's no HTML element involved, such as making something red and large. For that reason, class-based styles can be used again and again in the same page. A third type of style, ID-based styles, can be applied only once per Web page. Commonly used to style such items as columns and footers in layouts, ID-based styles are covered in Chapter 8 on page 147.

Using the CSS Tools

Expression Web comes loaded with tools to make creating and managing CSS easy. The Manage Styles task pane tab provides an at-a-glance spot for creating and organizing your styles (**Figure 7.1**). Its neighbor, the Apply Styles task pane tab, includes thumbnail previews of each style (**Figure 7.2**). The CSS Properties pane offers three ways to sort your CSS tags: a summary of all tags in the current selection, the cascade of which styles are subordinate to others, and a list of all the CSS rules, in alphabetical or categorical order (**Figure 7.3**).

Every style uses one of three selectors

Circled styles used in selected page

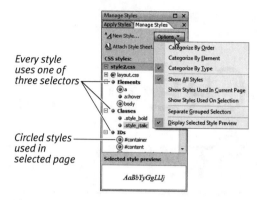

Figure 7.1 The Manage Styles tab provides an at-a-glance spot for creating and organizing your styles.

Show by alphabet *Show set rules at top* *Show all rules affecting selection*

Show by category

Tag selected

All rules applied to tag

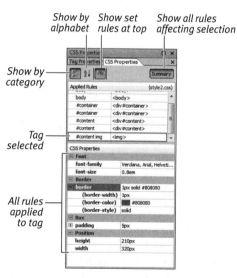

Figure 7.3 The CSS Properties pane offers several ways to sort through all your CSS properties.

Figure 7.2 The Apply Styles tab includes thumbnail previews of each style.

USING THE CSS TOOLS

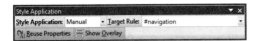

Figure 7.4 The Style Application toolbar is used mainly to build your CSS by hand.

Figure 7.5 The Style toolbar includes drop-down menus for applying classes and IDs.

Two toolbars can be used for CSS-related work as well, though I find the task panes more convenient. The Style Application toolbar is used mainly if you want to build all your CSS by hand in Manual mode (**Figure 7.4**). (If you're not a CSS code jockey, stick with the default Automatic mode.) The Style toolbar includes drop-down menus for applying classes and IDs, plus buttons to create a style or attach style sheets (**Figure 7.5**).

Yet another CSS tool, the CSS Reports pane, is covered separately on page 145.

To set up your CSS workspace:

1. Choose Task Panes, and make sure these task panes are turned on: Tag Properties, CSS Properties, Apply Styles, and Manage Styles.

2. Choose View > Visual Aids, and make sure that everything's turned on, except for the two ASP.NET choices.

3. Choose View > Quick Tag Selector. You're ready to start styling.

✔ Tip

- To display the CSS-related toolbars, choose View > Toolbars and pick Style Application or Style.

To change CSS preferences:

1. Choose Tools > Page Editor Options.

2. Click the CSS tab, and take a look at Expression Web's default settings. If you want to change any of them, use the drop-down menus.

How the Cascade Works

Why are they called *cascading* style sheets? It's because of the order in which the different styles exert control over items. The cascade runs, from top to bottom: external style sheet, internal style sheet, inline style.

The closer a tag sits to an item, the more precedence (or control) it has. So to put it another way: If there's no inline style for a particular item, then any rules for that type of item in the internal style sheet take command. If there are no rules for the item in the internal style sheet, then the external style sheet calls the shots. Used in combination, this style cascade gives you site-wide powers and single-paragraph precision.

The coding for the lowest level style type, inline, affects only a single paragraph or block. All the styling information sits within the paragraph's `<p>` and `</p>` tags. Internal style sheets give you styling control for a whole page. Its coding sits at the top of the html page between the `<head>` and `</head>` tags (**Figure 7.6**). External style sheets enable you to control styles across multiple pages or the entire site. As the name suggests, its coding sits in a separate file and controls any pages linked to it (**Figure 7.7**).

This chapter shows you how to create several types of styles and apply them to a single page. Some of those styles are then exported to an external style sheet. This approach lets you experiment on single pages before deciding which to apply sitewide. Many Web veterans, particularly those who know ahead of time exactly what styles they want to apply, prefer to code directly in an external style sheet. If that's your choice, jump straight to "To create a blank external style sheet" on page 140.

Figure 7.6 An internal style sheet's coding sits at the top of the page between the `<head>` and `</head>` tags.

Figure 7.7 Pages using external style sheets include a link to a separate file where all the styling codes reside.

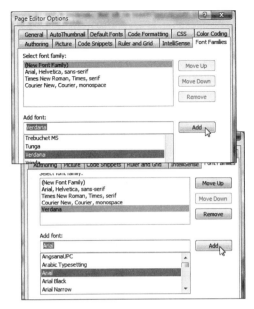

Figure 7.8 To create a font set, select (New Font Family) (top) and beginning adding to it one font at a time (bottom).

Creating Font Sets

It's the way of the Web that it doesn't matter how many cool fonts you have on your computer. What counts is what visitors to your site have on *their* computers. The standard workaround is to base your styles on specific *sets* of fonts. By default, Expression Web includes some very basic sets: a sans-serif, a serif, and a typewriter-style monospace, each of which includes some widely available fonts. You can create your own sets, listing left to right the order of the fonts to look for on visitors' computers. At the end of your list always add the appropriate basic set. That way, if your chosen fonts are not available, your set list will call up the common fonts or at least the appropriate typeface.

To create a font set:

1. Choose Tools > Page Editor Options, click the Font Families tab in the dialog box, and select (New Font Family) in the top list (top, **Figure 7.8**).

2. In the Add font box, type the first few letters of the font you want to use, and if it's on your computer, it automatically appears. Click Add (top, **Figure 7.8**).
   The font is added to the top list to start your new set (bottom, **Figure 7.8**).

3. Continue building your set font by font, by repeating step 2 until you're done (bottom, **Figure 7.8**).

(continued)

4. Use the Move Up and Move Down buttons to put your most-used font sets higher in the list (**Figure 7.9**). Click OK to close the dialog box.

The next time you create a style, the font-family drop-down menu includes your new sets in their new order (**Figure 7.10**).

✔ Tips

- To add fonts to an existing set, select it in step 2 and complete the rest of the steps. You cannot, however, reorder the fonts in the set.

- In step 2, you can add a font *not* on your computer by typing the full name. This is useful if you expect most computers to have that font installed—even if your computer does not.

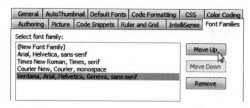

Figure 7.9 Use the Move Up and Move Down buttons to put your most-used font sets higher in the list.

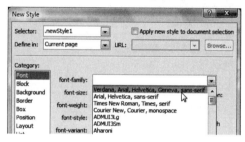

Figure 7.10 The next time you create a style, the font-family drop-down menu includes your new sets in their new order.

Figure 7.11 Use the Selector drop-down menu to choose h1 to set the appearance of every Heading 1.

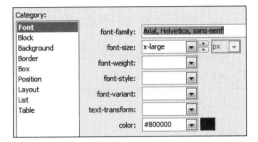

Figure 7.12 Use the Category choices and their related properties to set the appearance of your h1 heading.

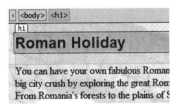

Figure 7.13 Any h1 items on the page assume the new style.

Creating Tag-based Styles

Tag-based styles affect every instance of a selected HTML element. Create an h1 CSS style once, for example, and it's applied to every h1 on that page (or the site if it's placed in an external style sheet). This section walks you through several types of elements, but the same steps can be applied to any HTML element.

To create heading-based styles:

1. Open any page in your Web site containing headings, and click the New Style button in the Manage Styles or Apply Styles tab.

2. In the New Style dialog box, use the Selector drop-down menu to choose h1 to set the appearance of every Heading 1 (**Figure 7.11**).

3. Use the Category choices and their related properties to set the appearance of your h1 headings (**Figure 7.12**). Click OK at the bottom of the dialog box to close it.

   The Manage Styles tab adds the h1 style to the Elements category, and any h1 items on the page assume the new style (**Figure 7.13**).

4. Repeat steps 1 through 3 for any other heading sizes you need.

CREATING TAG-BASED STYLES

✔ Tips

- Once you establish all your heading styles, the appropriate style is automatically applied whenever you resize a heading (**Figure 7.14**).

- If, as is common, you find yourself working on elements that are nested within elements, use the Quick Tag Select to click the right tag and immediately select everything that belongs with that tag (**Figure 7.15**).

- While it's common to set sizes based on pixels, using keywords (xx-small through xx-large) allows users to adjust, boost, or reduce the *overall* size of text items as needed. Instead of focusing on absolute pixel control, concentrate on establishing a clear hierarchy using the *relative* sizes of elements.

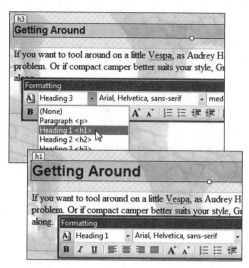

Figure 7.14 Once you establish all your heading styles, the appropriate style is automatically applied whenever you resize a heading.

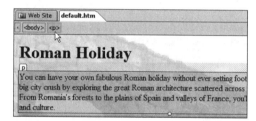

Figure 7.15 Use the Quick Tag Select to immediately select everything that belongs with that tag.

Figure 7.16 Use the Selector drop-down menu to choose a:link and set the appearance of an unvisited hyperlink.

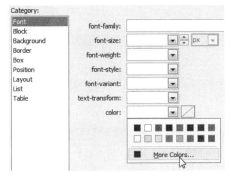

Figure 7.17 Leave the Category set to Font, click the color drop-down menu, and choose More Colors.

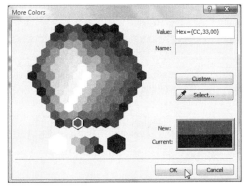

Figure 7.18 In the More Colors dialog box, pick a color, and click OK.

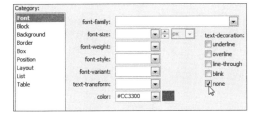

Figure 7.19 Select none in the text-decoration column so that the links will not be underlined.

To style hyperlinks:

1. Open any page in your Web site containing links, and click the New Style button in the Manage Styles or Apply Styles tab.

2. In the New Style dialog box, use the Selector drop-down menu to choose a:link to set the appearance of an unvisited hyperlink (**Figure 7.16**).

3. Leave the Category set to Font, click the color drop-down menu, and choose More Colors (**Figure 7.17**).

4. In the More Colors dialog box, pick a color and click OK (**Figure 7.18**).

5. When New Style dialog box reappears, select none in the text-decoration column so that the links will not be underlined (**Figure 7.19**). Click OK at the bottom of the dialog box to close it.

   The Manage Styles tab adds an Elements category listing the a:link style and any links in the page assume the new style (**Figure 7.20**).

(continued)

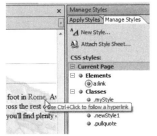

Figure 7.20 The Manage Styles tab adds an Elements category listing the a:link style and any links in the page assume the new style.

STYLING HYPERLINKS

6. Repeat steps 1 through 5, choosing a:hover in step 2 and a different color in step 4 (**Figure 7.21**). (It's common to leave hover links underlined.)

7. Repeat steps 1 through 5, choosing a:visited in step 2 and a third color in step 4 (**Figure 7.22**). Click OK to close the New Style dialog box for the last time.

The Manage Styles tab lists all three link styles (**Figure 7.23**). To export these styles to an external style sheet, see page 143.

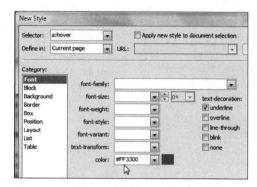

Figure 7.21 Choose a different color (right) for the a:hover link style and select underline.

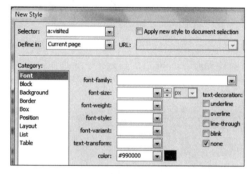

Figure 7.22 Choose a third color for the a:visited link style and reselect none again.

Figure 7.23 The Manage Styles tab lists all three link styles within the Elements category.

Figure 7.24 To create a class-based style in the example, start by selecting a paragraph to style.

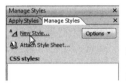

Figure 7.25 Click the New Style button in the Manage Styles or Apply Styles tab.

Figure 7.26 By default, the New Style dialog box names your first new style .newStyle1 and defines it in the current page.

Figure 7.27 Select the categories you want to style, and pick the properties for each.

Creating Class-based Styles

In contrast to element-based styles, whose use is tied to a specific tag such as h1, a class-based style can be applied to anything. Thanks to that flexibility, you'll probably change their appearance over time. For that reason, try to name them based on their function (`.caption` or `.pullquote`) rather than their appearance (`.thatcoolblue ihatedaweeklater`). See page 135 for how to rename a class-based tag without losing its original links.

To create a class-based style:

1. Open the Web page in which you want to create an internal style. In our example, we've selected a paragraph we want to style (**Figure 7.24**).

2. Click the New Style button in the Manage Styles or Apply Styles tab (**Figure 7.25**).

3. By default, the New Style dialog box names your first new style `.newStyle1` and defines it in the current page (**Figure 7.26**). Give it a name of your own, `myStyle` in this example. (Expression Web automatically adds the beginning period to preserve the class-based styling.)

4. Select the Font category and pick the properties you want to use (**Figure 7.27**). Set the properties for any other categories as needed. Use the preview area to fine-tune your choices, and click OK.

   The new style appears in the Manage Styles pane.

(continued)

5. To apply the style to the still unchanged paragraph, right-click the new style in the Manage Styles tab and choose Apply Style from the drop-down menu (left, **Figure 7.28**).

or

Switch to the Apply Styles tab and click the new style (right, **Figure 7.28**).

The selection changes to reflect the new styling, and the paragraph's tag now includes the style name <p.myStyle> (**Figure 7.29**).

✔ Tips

- Don't use a number at the start of a style name, such as .1stStyle. Expression Web will create the style but will not let you apply it.

- In step 4, for such common settings as Georgia, medium, and normal, just type the first few letters. Expression Web supplies the rest, eliminating the need to constantly click the drop-down menus.

- Internal style sheets are sometimes called embedded styles because all the coding is placed between the page's <head> and </head> tags.

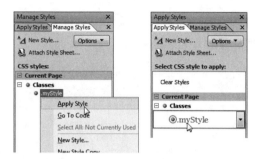

Figure 7.28 To apply a style, right-click it in the Manage Styles tab and choose Apply Style (left) or just click the new style in the Apply Styles tab (right).

Figure 7.29 The paragraph changes to reflect the new styling, and its tag includes the style name.

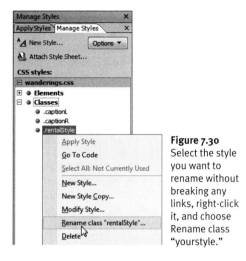

Figure 7.30
Select the style you want to rename without breaking any links, right-click it, and choose Rename class "yourstyle."

Figure 7.31 Type the new name, and click OK.

To rename a class-based style:

1. In either the Apply Styles or Manage Styles tabs, select the class-based style you want to rename while updating all references to it. Right-click it, and choose Rename class "yourstyle" from the drop-down menu (**Figure 7.30**).

2. Type the new name, and click OK (**Figure 7.31**).

   A status dialog box displays how many style references have been updated. Click OK to close the dialog box.

✔ Tip

- If you rename a class-based style in the Modify Style dialog box, any existing links will break. Use that dialog box to change the style's *properties,* not its name.

Creating Inline Styles

So you've set up your element-based and class-based styles. But what if you have a single paragraph you want to look a little different from all the others? That's where the inline class comes in. See "How the Cascade Works" on page 126 if you want to review how inline styles interact with style sheets.

To create an inline style:

1. Click anywhere inside the paragraph or block you want to style.

2. Click the New Style button in the Manage Styles or Apply Styles tab (**Figure 7.32**).

3. In the New Style dialog box, select (inline style), the very first item in the Selector drop-down menu (**Figure 7.33**).

4. Select a category on the left, and use the related drop-down menus to create a style (**Figure 7.34**). Use the preview area to gauge the effect, and click OK.

   The dialog box closes, and the style is applied to the selected paragraph or block (**Figure 7.35**).

✔ Tip

■ Expression Web provides two other clues that you've created an inline style: The CSS Properties tab calls it that, and it does *not* appear in the Manage Styles tab (**Figure 7.36**).

■ Don't confuse inline *styles* with inline *elements,* which are applied to just a few characters or words within a paragraph. An example of an inline element would be <em> emphasized </em> word.

Figure 7.32 As with other styles, the first step for creating an inline style is to click the New Style button.

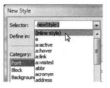

Figure 7.33 The difference comes when you then select (inline style) in the Selector drop-down menu.

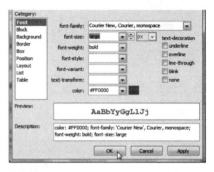

Figure 7.34 Select a category on the left, and use the related drop-down menus to create a style.

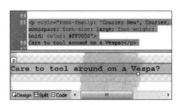

Figure 7.35 As the code at the top shows, the inline style is added *inside* the selected paragraph or block.

Figure 7.36 Two more clues that you've created an inline style: The CSS Properties tab calls it that, and it does *not* appear in the Manage Styles tab.

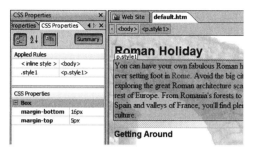

Figure 7.37 If you create a style that you really like...

Figure 7.38 ...it's easy to copy and apply elsewhere.

Figure 7.39 To copy and change a style, select it in the Manage Styles tab and choose New Style Copy.

Figure 7.40 Give the copy a new name in the Selector text box, and make any changes from the original style.

Figure 7.41 The modified style is added to the Manage Styles tab list.

Copying and Changing Styles

You can quickly create variations of a style by copying it and changing a property or two. Likewise, it's easy to modify an existing style as needed. In fact, it's common to create a class-based style and then realize that it'd work well as an element-based style. A typical example might involve getting a paragraph styled just so and then wanting to apply it to all your paragraphs by converting it to an element-based style (**Figures 7.37** and **7.38**).

If you accidentally apply a style or simply change your mind, it's easy to remove the styling from that element without deleting the style rule itself. Once a style's deleted, however, it's gone. So you may want to hold off a bit before deleting a style. You can always remove it from an element without deleting it entirely.

To copy and change a style:

1. In the Manage Styles tab, select the style you want to duplicate and choose New Style Copy from the drop-down menu (**Figure 7.39**).

2. In the New Style dialog box, give the copy a new name in the Selector text box, and make any changes from the original style (**Figure 7.40**).

3. Click OK.

   The dialog box closes, and the modified style is added to the Manage Styles tab list (**Figure 7.41**).

To convert a style:

1. Right-click the class-based style that you want to make into an element-based style (**Figure 7.42**).

2. In the Modify Style dialog box, use the Selector drop-down menu to choose the element you want to style (the **p** tag in this case) (**Figure 7.43**). Click OK.

   The dialog box closes, and all instances of that tag update automatically. The new element-based style also is listed in the Manage Styles tab.

✔ Tip

- The original custom class-based style remains, which you can delete or keep for later use.

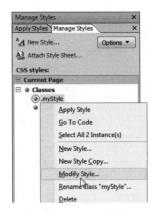

Figure 7.42 Right-click the class-based style that you want to convert to an element-based style, and choose the element in the drop-down menu.

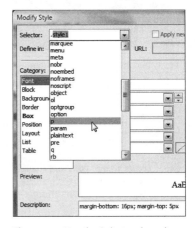

Figure 7.43 Use the Selector drop-down menu to choose the element you want to style (the p tag in this case).

Figure 7.44 Select the element whose style you want to remove.

Figure 7.45 In the Apply Styles tab, click the Clear Style button...

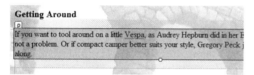

Figure 7.46 ...and the style is removed.

Figure 7.47 In the Apply Styles tab, right-click the style you want to delete and choose Delete.

To remove a style:

1. Select the element whose style you want to remove (**Figure 7.44**).

2. In the Apply Styles tab, click the Clear Style button (**Figure 7.45**).

   The style is removed from the selected element (**Figure 7.46**).

To delete a style:

1. In the Apply Styles tab, right-click the style you want to delete and choose Delete from the drop-down menu (**Figure 7.47**).

2. An alert dialog box asks you to confirm the action. Click Yes.

   The style is removed.

Creating Style Sheets

Internal style sheets are created automatically as you add styles to a Web page. Because all the coding is placed in the header section of the page, it applies only to that page (**Figure 7.48**). An external style sheet offers several advantages over each page carrying its own internal style sheet. The external sheet lets you easily apply styles across some or all of the pages in your Web site. It also speeds downloads since the CSS coding that would have been in each page's header is consolidated within the single external style sheet.

To create a blank external style sheet:

Do one of the following:

◆ Click the New button in the Common or Standard toolbars and choose CSS from the drop-down menu.

◆ Choose File > New > CSS.

◆ Choose File > New, and in the New dialog box, choose Page > General > CSS. Click OK (**Figure 7.49**).

A blank, untitled CSS file opens in the Editing window and is listed in the Manage Styles tab (**Figure 7.50**). See "To save a blank style sheet" on the next page.

Figure 7.48 Internal style sheets place all the style coding in the header section of the page.

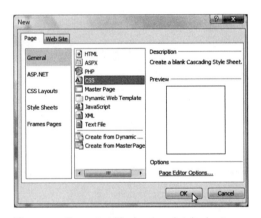

Figure 7.49 To create a blank external style sheet, choose Page > General > CSS in the New dialog box.

Figure 7.50 A blank, untitled CSS file opens in the Editing window (left), and is listed in the Manage Styles tab (right).

Figure 7.51 To save a blank style sheet, use the Save As dialog box to navigate to your current Web site (top). Give it a distinctive name, set the Save as type drop-down menu to CSS Files, and click Save (bottom).

Figure 7.52 The style sheet's new name appears in the Manage Styles tab.

To save a blank style sheet:

1. After a new, blank style sheet appears in the Editing window (see previous task), press ([Ctrl][S]).

2. Use the Save As dialog box to navigate to your current Web site (top, **Figure 7.51**). Give the style sheet a distinctive name, set the Save as type drop-down menu to CSS Files, and click Save (bottom, **Figure 7.51**). (See tip below.)

   The open page's tab displays the new name, as does its listing in the Manage Styles tab (**Figure 7.52**).

✔ Tip

- There's no standard practice for naming external style sheets. Common naming schemes include main.css, style1.css, global.css. To help me keep straight which style sheets goes with which site, I name the external style sheet after the site. Hence, in step 2 above, wanderings echoes the site's name.

To attach a style sheet to pages:

1. Open the page to which you want to attach an existing external style sheet. (The style sheet can be blank, as explained below.)

2. If the style sheet resides in the same Web site as the open page, click and drag it from the Folder List onto the page (**Figure 7.53**).

   or

   If the style sheet is stored outside the current site, click the Attach Style Sheet button in the Apply Styles or Manage Styles tabs (**Figure 7.54**). Use the Attach Style Sheet dialog box to browse to the sheet (**Figure 7.55**). Click OK.

   The page's Manage Styles tab now lists the external style sheet (**Figure 7.56**).

✔ Tips

- There are two ways to attach a style sheet to *multiple* pages at once: Ctrl-click the pages in the Folder List, and then click the Attach Style button as explained in step 2. Or when the Attach Style Sheet dialog box appears in step 2, select All HTML Pages.

- The Attach Style Sheet dialog box offers you the choice of attaching the style sheet as a link or an import (**Figure 7.55**). Links are more commonly used because more browsers support them. Imports, when placed inside a linked style sheet, offer a way to serve newer browsers without confusing older browsers. Older browsers will use the basic linked sheet, while newer browsers will import the more detailed style sheet.

- You also could attach a style sheet downloaded from one of the many Web sites that offer free example files. (See www.csszengarden.com for lots of inspiring, free samples.)

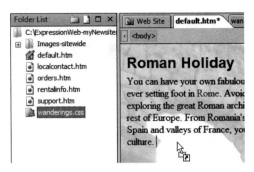

Figure 7.53 If a style sheet resides in the same site as the open page, click and drag it from the Folder List onto the page.

Figure 7.54 If a style sheet is stored outside the current site, click the Attach Style Sheet button in the Apply Styles or Manage Styles tabs.

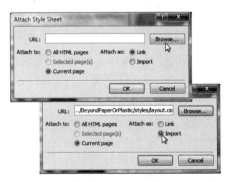

Figure 7.55 Use the Attach Style Sheet dialog box to link or import the style sheet.

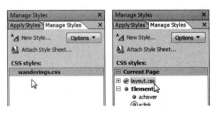

Figure 7.56 The page links to an external style sheet (left). The @layout.css signals that the page will import the style sheet if needed (right).

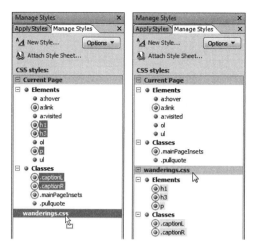

Figure 7.57 Select the internal styles you want used, and drag them onto the external sheet's name (left). The styles are added to the external style sheet (right).

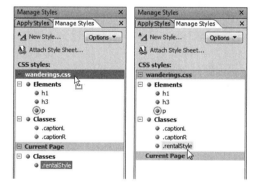

Figure 7.58 After attaching an external style sheet to another page, you can drag still more internal styles to the external sheet.

To move internal styles to an external style sheet:

1. First attach an external style sheet to the current page (see previous page), and then make sure that page's Manage Styles tab is open.

2. Click to select the internal styles you want used in the external sheet, and drag them onto the external sheet's name (left, **Figure 7.57**). (Use Ctrl-click to select multiple internal styles.) Release the cursor button.

   The styles are added to the external style sheet and are no longer listed as internal styles for the current page (right, **Figure 7.57**).

3. To add internal styles from *other* pages to the same external style sheet, attach the external style sheet to each of those pages. You can then click and drag styles from each internal page to the external style sheet (**Figure 7.58**).

✔ Tip

■ This method of adding internal styles from multiple pages allows you to build a master external style sheet very quickly.

143

To detach an external style sheet from a page:

1. Open the page from which you want to detach an external style sheet.

2. In the Manage Styles tab, right-click the external style sheet listing and choose Remove Link from the drop-down menu (**Figure 7.59**).

3. When the alert dialog box appears, click Yes. The link to the external style sheet is removed and no longer appears in the tab listing.

To detach an external style sheet from multiple pages:

1. In the Folder List, Ctrl-click to select all the pages from which you want to detach an external style sheet (**Figure 7.60**).

2. Choose Format > CSS Styles > Manage Style Sheet Links (**Figure 7.61**).

3. In Link Style Sheet dialog box, you have the option of removing the link from all the site's pages or of sticking with your selected pages only. Select the style sheet you want to detach, and click Remove (**Figure 7.62**). (In the example, there's only one link, but there could be multiple sheets.)

   The link to the external style sheet is removed. Unless there are other links you want removed, click OK to close the dialog box.

Figure 7.59 To detach an external style sheet from a page, right-click the external style sheet listing and choose Remove Link.

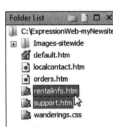

Figure 7.60 To detach an external style sheet from multiple pages, first Ctrl-click to select all the pages...

Figure 7.61 ...and then choose Format > CSS Styles > Manage Style Sheet Links.

Figure 7.62 Select the style sheet you want to detach, and click Remove.

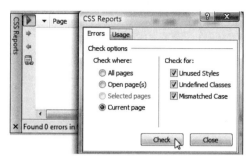

Figure 7.63 To run a CSS check, click the three-side arrow in the CSS Report pane's upper left, and select your report options in the CSS Reports dialog box.

Figure 7.64 The pane displays a list of possible problems.

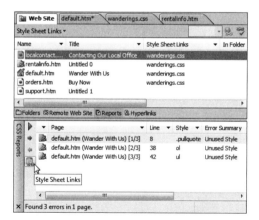

Figure 7.65 Click the Style Sheet Links button to inspect the style sheet controlling the style.

Solving CSS Problems

Expression Web's CSS Reports pane helps you trace CSS problems that could be hard to find otherwise. It can check if you have unused CSS styles, whether your pages include references to styles that you've failed to create, and mismatched references between your pages and styles. The task pane can then help you fix or delete the conflicts. Sometimes, however, the easiest way to find a problem is to use your eyeballs and the CSS Properties task pane. This is especially true when trying to sift through whether another part of a style cascade is inadvertently affecting an item. See "To track down CSS problems" on the next page.

To run CSS reports:

1. Open your Web site, and choose Task Panes > CSS Reports to display the CSS Reports task pane.

2. Click the three-side arrow in the pane's upper left, select your report options in the CSS Reports dialog box, and click Check (**Figure 7.63**).

   A list of possible problems is generated (**Figure 7.64**).

3. Click the smaller blue arrow next to each listing to see the coding that may be creating a problem (**Figure 7.64**).

   or

   Click the Style Sheet Links button to inspect the style sheet controlling the style (**Figure 7.65**).

4. Make changes as necessary and run the report again until you've completed the fixes.

✔ Tip

■ An unused style isn't really a problem. But if the report finds lots of them, delete them to keep your site uncluttered.

To track down CSS problems:

1. Select the item containing a style that's not working as expected. In our example, it's a style for controlling image insets. The image, which should be aligned with the top of the adjacent text, sits too low (right, **Figure 7.66**).

2. In the CSS Properties task pane, click the Summary and Show set properties on top buttons (left, **Figure 7.66**).

3. Look through the pane's right column for a property that could be causing the problem. In the example, the clear property is set to both.

4. If you suspect a particular property is causing the problem, select another property in the adjacent drop-down menu. In our example, we've changed the clear property to inherit (left, **Figure 7.67**).

   If the problem doesn't go away, reset the property and try another item. In our example, the change fixed the problem, and the image now aligns with the top of the text (right, **Figure 7.67**).

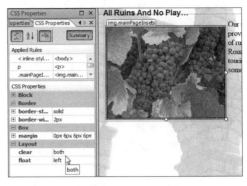

Figure 7.66 The CSS Properties task pane is great for tracking down problems like this image refusing to align with the top of the adjacent text.

Figure 7.67 Changing the clear property from both to inherit fixes the image alignment problem.

CREATING
LAYOUTS WITH CSS

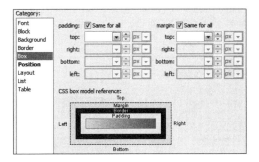

Figure 8.1 CSS positioning depends on the box model where each element is treated as a box positioned inside another box.

Cascading Style Sheets gives you so many options for controlling position-related properties that it can be overwhelming when you first start. That's especially true if you previously depended on tables for layouts. Whether it's a paragraph, an image, or a page division, CSS positioning treats all of these elements like boxes. You saw a preview of this box model working with image padding and margins in Chapter 5. Take another look at an image from that chapter to get a better sense for how the box model works (**Figure 8.1**). From the middle to the outside of the box, you have: an element's content, its surrounding padding, a border, and its margins. CSS applies that same boxes-in-boxes approach to position headers, sidebars, main columns, and such within page layouts. Combined with float and clear tags, which control how items are placed side by side, you can create precise, yet flexible, layouts for entire Web sites.

CSS layouts depend on two items working hand in glove: *div tags* (short for page divisions) and *ID-based styles*. Unlike the element- or class-based styles used in the previous chapter, ID-based styles can only be applied once per Web page. That limitation makes them ideal for styling such once-a-page items as navigation bars, mastheads, layout columns, and footers.

Positioning Properties

By default, a Web page displays elements in the natural top-to-bottom *flow* of its coding. CSS gives you five settings, or properties, to control any element's place in that flow: absolute, fixed, relative, static, and inherit. To get a better sense of how each property compares with the others, take a look at the accompanying screenshots of the Editing window and CSS Properties tab.

◆ **Absolute:** An absolutely positioned element is not confined by the page's code flow, and so, you can place it side-by-side with another element (**Figure 8.2**). That's because its position is dictated by its relation to its *parent* box, the body tag, which is usually pegged to the page's left-top corner (left, **Figure 8.2**). If you insert an absolutely positioned element *inside* another absolutely positioned element, its position is dictated by that *parent* element's position (**Figure 8.3**). In the first version of Expression Web, such elements did not always automatically expand to hold added content when viewed in a browser. However, Expression Web 2 has fixed the problem (**Figure 8.4**).

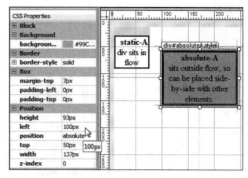

Figure 8.2 An absolutely positioned element is placed in relation to the page's left, top corner (0,0). Here absolute-A sits 100 pixels to the left and 50 pixels from the top of that corner spot. Its position has no effect on the static-A element.

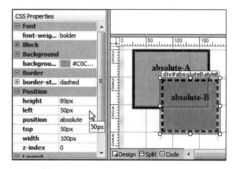

Figure 8.3 Child and parent relationships: absolute-B sits inside absolute-A, so its left-top position of 50, 50 is based on absolute-A's left-top position of 300, 25.

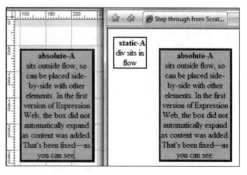

Figure 8.4 Expression Web has fixed the problem of browsers showing content spilling out of the layer container.

Figure 8.5 A fixed object's position is dictated by its relation to the browser *window,* so it sits in the same spot...

Figure 8.6 ...even as you scroll to the bottom of the page.

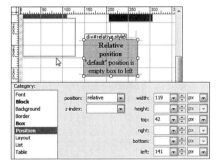

Figure 8.7 With a relatively positioned element, its left-top coordinates (141, 42) change relative to its normal spot in the code flow, marked here by the empty box.

◆ **Fixed:** The position of a fixed object is dictated by its relation to the browser *window* rather than the page or other objects. If you scroll the browser window up or down, the fixed object stays in the same place even as other page objects move in and out of the window (**Figures 8.5** and **8.6**).

◆ **Relative:** A relatively position page element remains part of a page's code flow, which means its placement will affect the layout of other nearby elements. When you move a relatively positioned element, its x-y coordinates change relative to its normal spot in the code flow (**Figure 8.7**).

◆ **Static:** A static object sits in the top-to-bottom code flow of the page. You can change its place in that flow (**Figure 8.8**). However, you cannot move it to the side of another element, since that falls outside the code flow (**Figure 8.9**). As explained in the next section, that aspect of positioning is controlled by the float and clear tags.

◆ **Inherit:** If you set an element's positioning to inherit, it simply uses the positioning of the enclosing parent element.

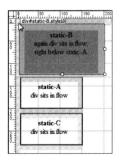

Figure 8.8 Static elements can be reordered in the top-to-bottom code flow, as here where static-B has been placed above static-A.

Figure 8.9 Static elements cannot be moved out of the code flow into a side-by-side position.

POSITIONING PROPERTIES

Using the Float and Clear Tags

While absolute positioning is precise, it's not very flexible. For a more liquid layout that can accommodate a variety of viewing devices, use the other four positioning properties in combination with the float and clear tags. Both tags can be found in the Layout category of the New Style and Modify Style dialog boxes (**Figures 8.10** and **8.11**). The float tag works similarly to the wrapping styles that control how text flows around images. If you apply a left float to an element, for example, the element shifts to the left side of its enclosing container, allowing other elements to wrap down the right side. Apply the clear tag to elements to control how they flow in response to nearby floated elements. In effect, you can override the default settings for where a new line break falls amid elements running down the side of a floated element.

Floating Properties

◆ **Left:** The element floats left, allowing other elements to flow down its right side (**Figure 8.12**).

◆ **None:** This is the default setting and causes the element to sit right where it falls in the flow. Other elements will not wrap around it. Most browsers respond to a blank property box as if it's set to none. Some browsers, however, can't read the blank. In those cases, select the None setting so that the browser renders the page properly.

◆ **Right:** The element floats right, allowing other elements to flow down its left side (**Figure 8.13**).

◆ **Inherit:** The element uses the float setting of its enclosing parent element.

Figure 8.10 The float tag can be applied in four ways.

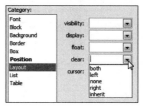

Figure 8.11 The clear tag offers five positioning choices.

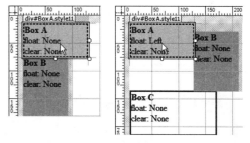

Figure 8.12 Changing the float on Box A from None (left) to Left (right) allows Box B to run down the right side. Box C doesn't shift right because Box B bumps it far enough down the page to sit under Box A.

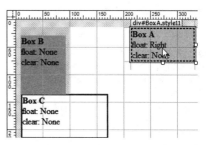

Figure 8.13 Box A floats to the right, allowing Box B to run down its left side.

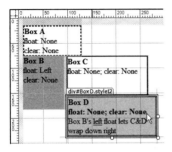

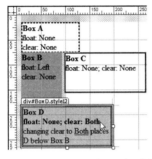

Figure 8.14 Top: Box D sits to the right because Box B, which is floated left, is deeper than Box C alone. Bottom: Changing Box D's clear tag from None to Both forces D to run on a new line because it blocks anything from running on either side of it.

Clearing Properties

◆ **Both:** Apply this to an element when you want to block floats on both sides. It forces other elements to run above or below it (**Figure 8.14**).

◆ **Left:** Apply this to an element to block other elements from floating to its left.

◆ **None:** Apply this to an element when it's OK for other elements to float on either side. As with float's none setting, use none when browsers don't recognize the default setting where the property box is blank.

◆ **Right:** Apply this to an element to block other elements from floating to its right.

◆ **Inherit:** Apply this to an element to use the clear setting of its enclosing parent element.

Using the Positioning Tools

Just as they did in formatting styles in Chapter 7, the Apply Styles, Manage Styles, and CSS Properties task panes play a big role in CSS positioning. Set them up beforehand to save yourself time.

To set up for positioning work:

1. Choose View > Ruler and Grid, and in the drop-down menu, select Show Ruler and Show Grid.

   Horizontal and vertical rulers appear along the top and left edges of the Editing Window, which is marked off with a thin line every 50 pixels.

2. Choose Task Panes, and make sure these task panes are turned on: Tag Properties, CSS Properties, Apply Styles, and Manage Styles.

3. Choose View > Visual Aids, and make sure that everything's turned on, except for the two ASP.NET choices.

4. Choose View > Quick Tag Selector.

   You're ready to start using CSS to position items on your Web pages.

✔ Tip

■ In step 1, if you want to use a unit other than pixels or change the grid spacing, choose View > Ruler and Grid > Configure, and make your changes.

Yesterday's Layout Tools: Frames, Tables, and Layers

If you're a fan of frames, layout tables, or layers, maybe the headline seems harsh. Back in the day, they filled a big gap in the Web's limited tool chest for creating half-decent layouts. Their shortcomings—framed pages cannot be bookmarked, layout tables generate oodles of tiny, transparent GIFs, and layers do not automatically adjust to their contents—were tolerated because there were few good choices. But just as new browsers support CSS positioning, and Expression Web is replacing FrontPage, so are these former layout stalwarts heading for the retirement pasture.

If you built, and still maintain, frame-based sites using FrontPage (or Dreamweaver for that matter), you'll find frames work very similarly in Expression Web. (You can reach them by choosing File > New > Page > Frames Pages). Likewise, FrontPage's layout tables are tucked inside Expression Web (Table > Layout Tables).

Despite its default placement next to the Apply Styles and Manage Styles tabs, the Layers tab should not play a big part in your CSS positioning work. While they're easy to draw and position, layers depend on absolute positioning and stacking, which can quickly make a hash of your layout. While layers still play a key role in creating such things as rollover-triggered navigation menus, you can create precise, complex layouts without them—as Expression Web's own prebuilt CSS layouts demonstrate in the next few pages.

Microsoft included all three tools to ease your eventual transition to building Web-standards-based pages using CSS. This chapter aims to help you do just that.

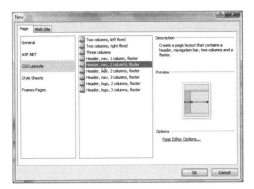

Figure 8.15 Select CSS Layouts in the left column and use the middle list and right-hand preview area to pick a layout.

Figure 8.16 The left_col division has a fixed width while the other divisions automatically match the page width.

Figure 8.17 In the CSS file, only three of the six ID names (#container, #left_col, and #page_content) start off with positioning properties.

Using Prebuilt CSS Layouts

Using the prebuilt CSS layouts included with Expression Web can spare you the inevitable trial and error that comes with building your own layouts from scratch. Be sure to open the tools and views explained in "Using the Positioning Tools" on the previous page.

To use prebuilt CSS layouts:

1. Choose File > New > Page.

2. In the New dialog box, select CSS Layouts in the left column and use the middle list and right-hand preview area to pick a page layout (**Figure 8.15**). Click OK.

   A new blank HTML-based page appears, along with a related untitled CSS-based page. In the example, the left-column division has a fixed width while the other divisions automatically match the page width (**Figure 8.16**). Switch to the new CSS file, and you can see that only three of the six ID names (#container, #left_col, and #page_content) start off with positioning properties (**Figure 8.17**).

3. Choose File > Save All.

4. Use the Save As dialog box to name and title the HTML page and its related external CSS file. By default, the CSS file is automatically attached to the HTML page. (In the example, we've named them prebuiltlayout.htm and prebuiltlayout.css.)

   (continued)

5. Add a bit of content to your page's major divisions—just a header or some text—to make the otherwise collapsed divisions easier to see (**Figure 8.18**).

6. Let's customize the ID-based styles to get a sense of how just a few settings can affect the layout of the divisions. Switch to the Manage Styles tab, right-click #left_col, and choose Modify Style (**Figure 8.19**).

7. In the Modify Style dialog box, boldfaced categories already have a property. In the #left_col example, Position is boldfaced because it's set to absolute with a width of 200 (pixels) (**Figure 8.20**). Change the width from 200 to 100, and click OK to close the dialog box.

8. In the Manage Styles tab, right-click #page_content, choose Modify Style, and select the Box category (**Figure 8.21**). Change the left margin from 200 to 100 and click OK to close the dialog box.

In the Web page, the left column and page content divisions shift to narrow the left column to half its original width, which also is reflected in the summary view of the CSS Properties tab (**Figure 8.22**).

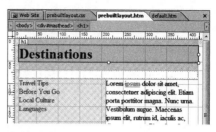

Figure 8.18 Add a bit of content to your page's major divisions to make the otherwise collapsed divisions easier to see.

Figure 8.19 Right-click #left_col, and choose Modify Style.

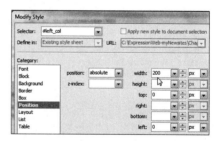

Figure 8.20 The #left_col division is preset to a width of 200 pixels.

Figure 8.22 The two layout divisions shift to narrow the left column to half its original width, which also is reflected in the CSS Properties tab.

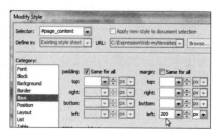

Figure 8.21 Change the left margin for #page_content from 200 to 100 pixels.

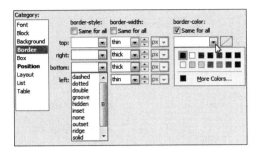

Figure 8.23 You can start styling the look of each division by changing properties such as the borders.

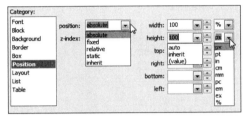

Figure 8.24 Naturally enough, the Position category controls many of the CSS positioning properties.

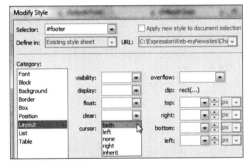

Figure 8.25 The Layout category handles the float and clear tags, which control side-by-side positioning of elements.

9. As you did in Chapter 7, you can start styling the look of the ID-based divisions themselves, such as the borders (**Figure 8.23**). However, hold off styling the *content* of the divisions (heads, text, lists, and so on) until you read "Using Contextual Selectors" on page 156.

10. Continue using the Modify Style dialog box to customize each division, paying particular attention to the position-related categories: Box, Position, and Layout (**Figures 8.24** and **8.25**).

11. When you're done, choose File > Save All to preserve your changes to the HTML and CSS files. To use the layout with other pages, attach it to pages as you would any external style sheet.

✔ Tips

- The common naming convention for CSS files controlling layout is `layout.css`.

- To keep things relatively simple, the examples use just one CSS file. It's common for commercial Web sites, however, to have multiple, interlocking style sheets that use CSS coding hacks to work around the rendering problems of older browsers. If you want to learn more, dive in at these two great sites: `http://www.positioniseverything.net` and `http://alistapart.com`.

Using Contextual Selectors

As you saw in the previous section, the combination of div tags and ID-based styles enables you to create specific styles for your divisions. With the addition of contextual selectors, you can create styles that only appear when particular tags are used in specific divisions. Want a specially styled h3 header for a sidebar but nowhere else? How about a particular alignment-margin-padding combination for paragraphs in your main content division? Contextual selectors let you do it—without cluttering up your pages with lots of code. By moving the styles to an external style sheet, you also can quickly apply them to any pages laid out with those same divisions.

To create contextual selectors:

1. Click New Style in the Manage Styles tab. The New Style dialog box's selector field automatically generates a generic style name (top, **Figure 8.26**).

2. Press Backspace twice to get rid of that name and the period in front of it. Now type: #yourdivision_name(space) class_name. In the example, it's: #page_content p to create a style that's applied automatically to any paragraphs in the main page content area (bottom, **Figure 8.26**).

3. Set properties in the various categories in the Modify Style dialog box to create exactly the paragraph style you want (**Figure 8.27**). Click Apply if you want to see the effect and make adjustments, or click OK to close the dialog box.

   All the paragraph text in the division assumes the new style, and the contextual ID-based style is listed in the Manage Styles tab (**Figure 8.28**).

Figure 8.26 To create a contextual selector, replace the generic name (top) with your own version of #your-division_name(space) class_name.

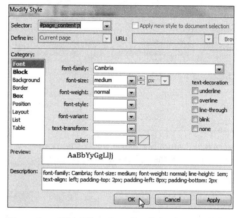

Figure 8.27 Click OK to close the dialog box, or click Apply to see the setting's effect and make adjustments.

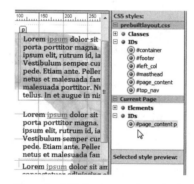

Figure 8.28 All the paragraph text in the division assumes the new contextual style, which is listed in the Manage Styles tab.

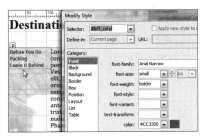

Figure 8.29 A contrasting p style is created for the left_col division.

Figure 8.30 Here a specific h3 style is used in the left column, and an h2 style for the main page content.

Figure 8.31 Click and drag the current page's ID styles to your external style sheet.

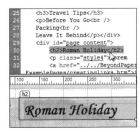

Figure 8.32 Contextual selectors don't clutter up the h2 tag in the Code view.

4. Repeat steps 1 through 3 to create a contextual style for paragraphs used in another page division.

In the example, a contrasting text style is created for the left column (**Figure 8.29**).

5. Repeat steps 1 through 3, only this time create contextual styles for the headers in your divisions. In the example, they are: `#left_col h3` and `#page_content h2` (**Figure 8.30**).

6. Click and drag the current page's ID styles to your external style sheet (**Figure 8.31**). (See page 140, if you need information on creating external style sheets.)

7. Choose File > Save All to preserve your work.

✔ Tips

- In step 2, if you reposition the New Style dialog box on your screen, you'll know the exact ID name to type because all the IDs can be seen in the Manage Styles tab.

- Switch over to Code view for any of these pages, and you'll see that the element tags remain clean and that all the styling information sits in the external style sheet (**Figures 8.32** and **8.33**).

Figure 8.33 All the contextual styling information for the h2 tag sits in the external style sheet.

Creating CSS Layouts from Scratch

No matter how nice the prebuilt layouts may be, at some point you may want to create your own CSS-based layouts. Be sure to first work a bit with the prebuilt CSS layouts to get comfortable with the process. Our from-scratch example is deliberately simple just to get you going. It's a two-step process: first you create the ID-based styles you'll want for each division, and then you create the divisions and pair them to those ID-based styles. By the way, some of the example styles are a bit garish so they show up better in the black-and-white screenshots. For your own examples, feel free to exhibit better taste. Adjust your workspace as explained in "To set up for positioning work" on page 152.

To create ID styles for a CSS layout:

1. Create a new blank HTML page ([Ctrl][N]) and a new blank CSS file (File > New > CSS).

2. Save both pages, naming them default.htm and layout.css.

3. Select the default.htm page, and click Attach Style Sheet in the Manage Styles tab. Use the Attach Style Sheet dialog box to navigate to the layout.css file (**Figure 8.34**). Click OK.

    The dialog box closes, and the page's Manage Styles tab now lists the external style sheet (**Figure 8.35**).

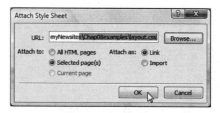

Figure 8.34 Use the Attach Style Sheet dialog box to navigate to the layout.css file.

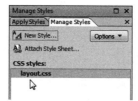

Figure 8.35 Once attached, the external style sheet is listed in the Manage Styles tab.

Figure 8.36 Replace the generic style name with: #container (#yourDivisionName).

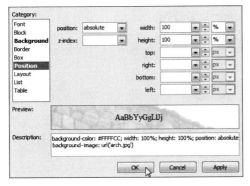

Figure 8.37 Because the container division encloses all the other page content, use the settings: position: absolute, width: 100%, and height: 100%.

Figure 8.38 The #container ID now is listed in the Manage Styles tab, though the dot is not circled because the ID has not been applied yet.

4. Click New Style in the Manage Styles tab. The New Style dialog box's selector field automatically generates a generic style name (top, **Figure 8.36**). Press [Backspace] twice to clear the field, and type: #container. Select Existing style sheet in the Define in drop-down menu and layout.css in the URL box (bottom, **Figure 8.36**).

5. With the New Style dialog box still open, set the Position category to position: absolute, width: 100%, and height: 100% (**Figure 8.37**). Set any other categories and properties you need, but remember that you also can add them later if needed. (For help on setting the position-related properties, see "Positioning Properties" on page 148.) Click OK.

The #container ID now is listed in the Manage Styles tab (**Figure 8.38**). Notice that the red dot is not circled because the ID has not been applied to a page yet.

(continued)

6. Repeat steps 4 and 5 to add the other division IDs you expect to need in your layout. You'll use them in the next task, "To insert div tags and pair with ID styles" (**Figure 8.39**).

7. When you're done, choose File > Save All. You can examine the properties for each ID style by switching to the Apply Styles tab or the style sheet (layout.css) (**Figures 8.40** and **8.41**).

✔ Tips

■ In step 5, by defining the container div as the page's full width and height, it's much easier to insert the rest of the divs on the page. The other advantage of putting all the other div tags inside the container div is that you can apply styles to all those divs just by modifying the container's styles. (For more information, see "Using Contextual Selectors" on page 156.)

■ In step 6, you do not need to do more than create the IDs for now. Unlike the example, you can do the detailed styling at any time.

Figure 8.39 Create the other ID-based styles you expect to need in your layout.

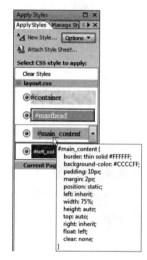

Figure 8.40 The Apply Styles tab offers visual reminders of each style, with the details available with a cursor roll over.

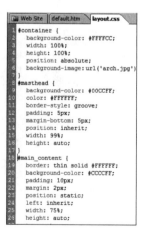

Figure 8.41 You also can inspect the details of your styles by switching to the style sheet.

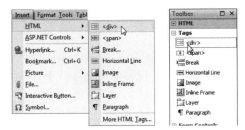

Figure 8.42 To insert div tags, choose Insert > HTML > <div> (left) or double-click the div button in the Toolbox pane (right).

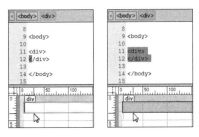

Figure 8.43 The empty division is marked by a dotted border (left). To select the div, click on it in the Design window, Code window, or the Quick Tag Selector at the top of the Editing window (right).

Figure 8.44 To pair a div with an ID-based style, make a selection from the id drop-down menu in the Tag Properties tab.

Figure 8.45 The container id is applied to the div tag in the Tag Properties pane as well in the Quick Tag selector and page views.

To insert div tags and pair with ID styles:

1. Click anywhere inside the HTML page used in the previous task (default.htm).

2. Add a div tag to the page by choosing Insert > HTML > <div> or double-clicking the div button in the Toolbox pane (**Figure 8.42**). The div button also can be found in the Common toolbar.

   An empty division, marked by a dotted border, appears across the top of the page (left, **Figure 8.43**).

3. To select the div, click its box in the Design window, or any part of <div></div> in the Code window, or the <div> tag in the Quick Tag Selector at the top of the Editing window (right, **Figure 8.43**).

4. Switch to the Tag Properties pane, which sits in the same task pane as the CSS Properties pane, and click the blank column to the right of id. A list of the IDs you previously created appears in the drop-down menu (**Figure 8.44**). Choose container, and press ⏎Enter.

   The container id is applied to the div tag in the Tag Properties pane, as well in the Quick Tag selector and page views (**Figure 8.45**). This step is the key to the CSS and HTML files working in tandem.

   (continued)

5. Using the Design or Code window, click *inside* the container div. Repeat steps 2 through 4 to insert and ID the next division for your page. In the example, it's div#masthead (**Figure 8.46**).

6. Because the masthead div now sits inside the container div, use the Split view to make it easier to keep the next div also *inside* the container div. Click just before the container div's end tag </div> (**Figure 8.47**).

7. Repeat steps 2 through 4 until you insert divs to pair with all the IDs you generated in "To create ID styles for a CSS layout" on page 158.

8. Choose File > Save All to preserve your work. You now can either go back and further modify the styling for the IDs, add content to the divisions, or create contextual selectors tied to those IDs as explained on page 156 (**Figure 8.48**).

✔ Tips

■ If you're working in Split view, changes made in the Design view simultaneously appear in the Code view. However, changes made in Code view do not show up in the Design view until you refresh the view ([F5]) or save the page ([Ctrl][S]).

■ In step 5, you could insert the divs in any order. But if you order them top-to-bottom as they would appear on your page, it'll be easier for non-CSS browsers, such as those in cell phones, to render the layout correctly.

■ While the CSS Properties tab and Manage Styles tab are your best tools for changing a division's positioning, the Positioning toolbar can speed your work by providing at-a-glance information about key aspects of positioning (**Figure 8.49**).

Figure 8.46 The masthead division should be inserted *inside* the container division's tag.

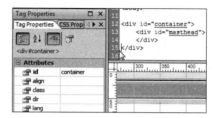

Figure 8.47 To insert another division inside the container, click *between* the masthead's end tag (the first </div>) and the container's end tag (the second </div>).

Figure 8.48 The end result: a from-scratch CSS-based layout, complete with contextual selectors.

Figure 8.49 The Positioning toolbar can speed your work with key information about positioning.

ADDING
BEHAVIORS & MEDIA

One of the great advantages of Web pages over printed pages is their ability to respond to viewers' actions. Triggered by a cursor motion or click, buttons can change colors, images can swap out, and messages can pop up. Of course, such behaviors can cut both ways, driving away instead of inviting visitors. When used with restraint and clear purpose, however, interactivity can beckon viewers to stick around and further explore your site.

One of the big improvements in Expression Web 2 is the ability to add Flash, Windows Media, and even Microsoft's new Silverlight-based plug-ins. Though the details of Silverlight are not covered in this beginning/intermediate level book, the chapter does explain how to insert Silverlight-based media into your pages.

Creating Interactive Buttons

Expression Web makes it a breeze to generate professional looking buttons that interact with the visitor's cursor. Even better, you can go back and edit their style and labels at any time, and replacement images are generated automatically. If you're looking to create a row of buttons with the same look and height, be sure to see "To duplicate interactive buttons" on page 167

To add an interactive button:

1. In Design view, click on the page where you want to add a button. Choose Insert > Interactive Button (**Figure 9.1**).

2. In the Interactive Buttons dialog box, pick a style from the middle Buttons list, type a Text label, and click Browse (**Figure 9.2**).

3. Navigate to the page to which you want to link and type the text you want to display when a cursor hovers over the link (ditto for the Screen Tip button) (**Figure 9.3**). Click OK. (If the label doesn't fit the size, see step 3 of "To edit an interactive button" on page 166.)

4. When the Interactive Buttons dialog box reappears with the link added, click the Font tab (**Figure 9.4**).

5. In the Font tab, use the middle scroll boxes to choose your font, its style, and its size (**Figure 9.5**). (See second tip.)

Figure 9.1 To add an interactive button, choose Insert > Interactive Button.

Figure 9.2 Pick a style from the middle Buttons list, type a Text label, and click Browse.

Figure 9.3 Navigate to your target page, add the text you want to display when a cursor hovers over the link, and click OK.

Figure 9.4 When the Interactive Buttons dialog box reappears with the link added, click the Font tab.

Figure 9.5 Use the middle scroll boxes to choose your font, its style, and its size.

Figure 9.6 Test the hover and pressed color changes using your cursor in the top preview area

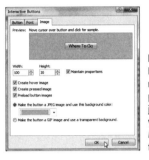

Figure 9.7 In the Image tab, you can resize the button proportionally or in just one dimension if you uncheck the Maintain proportions box.

Figure 9.8 The Save Embedded Files dialog box lets you choose where the new button images will be saved.

Figure 9.9 The button as it appears in the page's navigation-bar division.

Figure 9.10 Tested in the browser, the cursor rollover displays the text entered in step 2.

6. In the bottom half of the dialog box, set the colors you want the text to display based on the visitor's cursor action, plus the text's alignment. You can test the hover and pressed color changes in the top preview area (**Figure 9.6**).

7. Click the Image tab.

8. In the Image tab, you can enlarge or shrink the button itself, either proportionally or in just one dimension if you uncheck the Maintain proportions box (**Figure 9.7**). Change the background color for the JPEG image if you want, or select the second radio button if you'd rather use a GIF image. Click OK.

9. The Save Embedded Files dialog box shows where the new button images will be saved (**Figure 9.8**). Since each button generates three images, keep your images folder uncluttered by clicking Change Folder to create a buttons subfolder. When the dialog box reappears, click OK.

    The button appears in the page (**Figure 9.9**). Save your work and press F12 to test it in your browsers (**Figure 9.10**).

✔ Tips

■ Unlike the Insert Hyperlink dialog box, the Edit Hyperlink dialog box does not have a Create New Hyperlink button (**Figure 9.3**). So you'll want to create a destination page—à blank page will work fine and not interrupt your work—before you insert the button.

■ In step 5, don't worry about which fonts your site's visitors have installed on their machines. Since Expression Web creates *images* of the buttons, you can go wild.

To edit an interactive button:

1. Right-click a button you want to change, and choose Button Properties in the drop-down menu (**Figure 9.11**).

2. When the Interactive Buttons dialog box appears, use the Button tab to change the button's style, text label, or link (**Figure 9.12**). In the example, a new label is cut off on both ends (**Figure 9.13**).

3. Click the Image tab.

4. In the Image tab, uncheck the Maintain proportions box (top, **Figure 9.14**). Press the up arrow for the Width box to grow the label enough to show all the text (bottom, **Figure 9.14**). (See the tip.)

5. If you want to change the font, switch to the Font tab and make your changes. Otherwise, click OK to close the dialog box.

6. The Save Embedded Files dialog box shows where the new button images will be saved and warns you which previous images it will overwrite (**Figure 9.15**). Click OK.

   The button appears in the page. Save your work and press F12 to test it in your browsers.

✔ Tip

■ In step 4, if you increase either dimension but don't uncheck the Maintain proportions box, the whole image grows. That will create a height mismatch if the button is part of a row of buttons.

Figure 9.11 To edit an interactive button, right-click it and choose Button Properties.

Figure 9.12 Use the Button tab to change the button's style, text label, or link.

Figure 9.13 The new label is cut off on both ends, so click the Image tab.

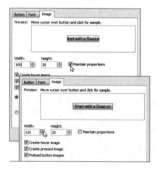

Figure 9.14 Uncheck Maintain proportions (top), and press the up arrow for the Width box to grow the label enough to show all the text (bottom).

Figure 9.15 The Save Embedded Files dialog box warns you about which previous images it will overwrite.

Figure 9.16 Right-click a button whose look you want to duplicate, and choose Copy.

Figure 9.17 Click where you want to add a matching button (just right of first button), and then right-click and choose Paste.

Figure 9.18 Right-click the duplicated button, and choose Button Properties to edit its label, link, and width.

Figure 9.19 Copying and pasting buttons makes it easy to populate navigation bars, even when you have to edit the labels and links.

To duplicate interactive buttons:

1. In Design view, right-click a button whose appearance you want to duplicate and choose Copy from the drop-down menu (**Figure 9.16**).

2. Click on the page where you want to add a matching button, typically in a row of buttons. Right-click and choose Paste from the drop-down menu (**Figure 9.17**).

   A copy of the button is pasted into the page, at which point you can right-click it and choose Button Properties to edit the label, link, and width (**Figure 9.18**).

✔ Tips

■ This is the quickest way to create matching buttons because the Font tab in the Interactive Button dialog box doesn't remember which font or size you used last.

■ You can paste a button on another page as well, which makes it easy to populate your site's navigation bars (**Figure 9.19**). Another option, of course, is to copy the entire row of buttons and paste it elsewhere, though it can be tricky making an accurate selection and finding the precise insert spot.

DUPLICATING INTERACTIVE BUTTONS

Adding Behaviors to Elements

Like interactive buttons, behaviors offer a way to create pages that respond to your users. Behaviors are driven by scripts that have two parts: an *action* triggered by a specific *event*. An example might be a sound that plays (the action) when a cursor rolls over an image (the event) (**Figures 9.20** and **9.21**). Behaviors can be applied to a variety of elements on the page, though not every behavior is possible with every element. For example, you cannot swap an image for another unless you've selected an image as your element. While the example below applies to swapping an image, the steps are essentially the same for adding any behavior. See **Table 9.1** on page 175 for a list of all the behavior choices. Beginners can quickly create interactive jump menus.

To add a behavior:

1. To open the Behaviors task pane, choose Format > Behaviors or choose Task Panes > Behaviors.

2. In Design view, click the element to which you want to add a behavior.

   The tag appears at the top of the Behaviors task pane (**Figure 9.22**).

3. In the Behaviors task pane, click Insert and choose an *action* from the drop-down menu. In the example, it's Swap Image (**Figure 9.23**).

Figure 9.20 The Behaviors task pane's Insert button lists available actions for the selected tag. Actions inappropriate for the element are dimmed.

Figure 9.21 Once you insert an *action* for a selected element (di v#masthead in this example), use the drop-down menu to pick a triggering *event*.

Figure 9.22 The tag for any selected element appears in the Behaviors task pane.

Figure 9.23 In the Behaviors task pane, click Insert and choose an *action* from the drop-down menu.

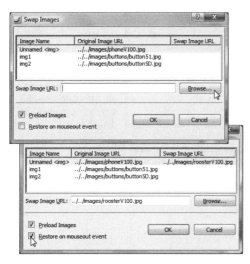

Figure 9.24 A dialog box lets you set the action's details. Here, the Swap Images dialog box asks you to browse to the image you want to swap in.

Figure 9.25 The Behaviors task pane lists the events and actions linked to that element.

Figure 9.26 An image swap behavior as tested in the browser: The first image appears (top) before the cursor rolls over the area, triggering a swap to the second image (bottom).

4. A dialog box appears to set the details of the action. Here, the Swap Images dialog box asks you to browse to the image you want to swap in (top, **Figure 9.24**). By selecting Restore on mouseout event, the swapped image appears only when a cursor hovers over the spot (bottom, **Figure 9.24**). Click OK to close the dialog box.

The Behaviors task pane lists the event and action now linked to that element. In the example, the image swaps in another image (the action) when the mouse moves over the element (the event) and restores the original (another action) when the mouse moves out (another event) (**Figure 9.25**).

5. Save your work, and test the page in a browser (**Figure 9.26**).

✔ Tips

- The Behaviors task pane lists events and actions in the order they occur. In step 4, the first event-action set (onmouseout and image restore) comes first because the page starts off that way. It's only after that event that the second event-action (onmouseover and image swap) would occur.

- If the event-action sets cannot be reordered, the up and down arrows remain dimmed.

- The available behaviors for elements are tied to the CSS schema you selected in the Authoring tab of the Page Editor Options dialog box. (Choose Tools > Page Editor Options.)

To change a behavior:

Do one of the following:

◆ Double-click any listed *action* to open its dialog box, where you can change the action's properties (**Figure 9.27**).

◆ Click the drop-down menu for any listed *event*, choose a new event, and release the cursor (**Figure 9.28**).

The new event replaces the original event in the Behaviors task pane.

◆ Click any listed *action,* and click Delete at the top of the Behaviors task pane (top, **Figure 9.29**).

The action disappears from the Behaviors task pane (bottom, **Figure 9.29**).

Figure 9.27 To change an *action*, double-click any listing to open its dialog box.

Figure 9.28 To change an *event*, use the drop-down menu to choose a new event.

Figure 9.29 Select an action in the Behaviors task pane, click Delete, and it is removed.

Figure 9.30 To go to another Web page, click Insert and choose Go To URL.

Figure 9.31 Browse to the URL you want to use, and click OK to close the dialog box.

Figure 9.32 To change the default event for the Go To URL action, make another choice in the drop-down menu.

To go to another Web page:

1. Select the page element you want to use. In the Behaviors task pane, click Insert and choose Go To URL (**Figure 9.30**).

2. When the dialog box appears, browse to the URL you want to use (**Figure 9.31**). Click OK to close the dialog box.

   The action is added to the Behaviors task pane with onmouseover as the default event setting (**Figure 9.32**).

3. If you'd rather use another triggering event, click the Events drop-down menu to change it. In the example, onclick gives the user more control than onmouseover.

4. Save your work and test the page in your browsers.

To check the browser version:

1. Click anywhere in the page. In the Behaviors task pane, click Insert and choose Check Browser.

2. In the dialog box that appears, select a browser from the first drop-down menu and then a version in the second drop-down menu (**Figure 9.33**).

3. Use the Browse button to set the first Go to URL text box to link to a page designed to look best for the browser selected in step 2.

4. Set the second Go to URL text box to link to another page designed to work well with all other browsers. Click OK to close the dialog box.

    The action is added to the Behaviors task pane with onclick as the default event setting.

5. If you'd rather use another triggering event, select it from the Events drop-down menu.

6. Save your work and test the page in your browsers.

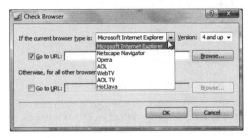

Figure 9.33 Select a browser from the first drop-down menu and then a version in the second drop-down menu.

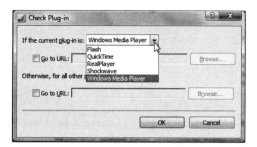

Figure 9.34 Select a media player plug-in from the drop-down menu.

To check for media plug-ins:

1. Before adding the behavior, create or import into your site the page containing the video or sound file you want to offer visitors. Back in your main Web page, add a small button, image, or bit of text to highlight the link to the media file. (Short, obvious wordings such as *Listen* or *Watch* get the job done).

2. In the Behaviors task pane, click Insert and choose Check Plug-in.

3. In dialog box that appears, select a media player plug-in from the drop-down menu (**Figure 9.34**).

4. Use the Browse button to set the first Go to URL text box to link to a multimedia item designed to look best for the plug-in selected in step 2.

5. Set the second Go to URL text box to link to another page designed to work well with all other media players. Click OK to close the dialog box.

   The action is added to the Behaviors task pane with onmouseover as the default event setting.

6. If you'd rather use another triggering event, select it from the Events drop-down menu.

7. Save your work and test the page in your browsers.

To create a popup message window:

1. Select the page element you want to use. In the Behaviors task pane, click Insert and choose Popup Message.

2. When the dialog box appears, type your message (**Figure 9.35**). Click OK to close the dialog box.

   The action is added to the Behaviors task pane with onmouseover as the default event setting.

3. If you'd rather use another triggering event, select it from the Events drop-down menu.

4. Save your work, and test the page in your browsers (**Figure 9.36**).

✔ Tip

■ If you absolutely must get visitors' attention, this is your tool. Otherwise, use with great restraint. A better option would be to use a status bar text message, as explained on the next page.

Figure 9.35 To create a popup message window, type your message.

Figure 9.36 Rolling the cursor over the Roman Holiday heading triggers the popup message.

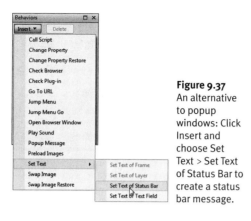

Figure 9.37 An alternative to popup windows: Click Insert and choose Set Text > Set Text of Status Bar to create a status bar message.

Figure 9.38 Type the message you want to appear in the browser's status bar.

To create a status bar message:

1. Select the page element you want to use. In the Behaviors task pane, click Insert and choose Set Text > Set Text of Status Bar (**Figure 9.37**).

2. When the dialog box appears, type your message (**Figure 9.38**). Click OK to close the dialog box.

   The action is added to the Behaviors task pane with onlick as the default event setting.

3. If you'd rather use another triggering event, select it from the Events drop-down menu.

4. Save your work, and test the page in your browsers.

Table 9.1

Available behaviors

NAME	WHAT IT DOES
Call Script	Enables you to trigger a custom JavaScript created outside Expression Web.
Change Property*	Enables you to change details of the behavior, depending on the behavior selected.
Change Property Restore	Reverts to previous property, based on event you choose.
Check Browser	Checks which browser and version the site's visitor is using. Enables you to serve special pages, including style sheets, based on those results.
Check Plug-in*	Checks if site's visitor has such things as Flash player installed. Enables you to serve different versions of pages based on those results.
Go To URL	Opens a link in either the existing page or in a new window.
Jump Menu	Enables you to create a drop-down menu of links that user can choose.
Jump Menu Go	Based on selected event trigger, sends user to the selected URL in a specified jump menu.
Open Browser Window	Enables you to open a new browser window, whose size and toolbars you specify.
Play Sound	Based on selected event trigger, causes browser to play selected sound.
Popup Message	Based on selected event trigger, causes browser to display a specific message in a popup window.
Preload Images	Allows background loading of secondary images for image swaps (rollovers).
Set Text	Displays specified text in a specific frame, layer, text field, or the status bar.
Swap Image	Based on selected event trigger, replaces one image with another.
Swap Image Restore	Restores the original image used before a Swap Image behavior replaced it.

*Requires Internet Explorer 5 or later, or Netscape 6 or later

CREATING A STATUS BAR MESSAGE

To open another browser window:

1. Select the page element you want to use, typically a link or image. In the Behaviors task pane, click Insert and choose Open Browser Window.

2. When the Open Browser Window dialog box appears, enter the URL or click Browse to set the contents of the new window (**Figure 9.39**).

3. Enter a window name and size. The window name does not appear in the new window. It's simply used as part of a generated script, so it cannot have any spaces or nonstandard ASCI characters.

4. Select the attributes you want to appear with the new window. At a minimum include: Navigation toolbar, Scrollbars as needed, and Resize handles. Click OK to close the dialog box.

   The action is added to the Behaviors task pane with onlick as the default event setting.

5. If you'd rather use another triggering event, select it from the Events drop-down menu.

6. Save your work, and test the page in your browsers (**Figure 9.40**).

✔ Tips

- As with popup messages, this behavior can test the patience of visitors if it simply bumps them into a whole new screen-gobbling window. It's more effective when used for small windows showing such things as a product detail or close-up view of something on the original page.

- Give your users a clue as to what will happen by adding an explanation in the image's alt text label (**Figure 9.40**).

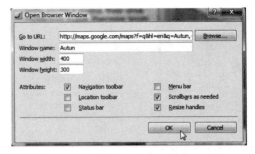

Figure 9.39 When setting another browser window to open, keep it small using the width and height text boxes. Always include resize handles so the user can control the new window.

Figure 9.40 When a cursor rolls over the photo (lower right), its alt text tells the user that a click will open a new window (upper left).

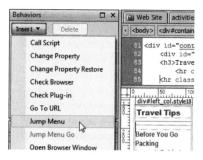

Figure 9.41 Click in the page where you want the menu to appear (right), and choose Jump Menu from the Insert drop-down menu in the Behaviors task pane (left).

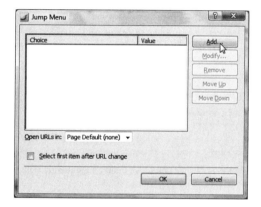

Figure 9.42 When the Jump Menu dialog box appears, click Add to begin building the menu list.

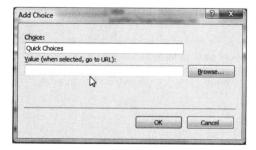

Figure 9.43 For the menu's first item, type a label to orient the visitor but leave the Value text box blank.

Using Jump Menus

A jump menu is one of the most useful of the many behaviors you can add to a page because it gives your users a lot of navigational information in a small space. By clicking the menu, users can choose among a variety of links to which they can jump directly.

To insert a jump menu:

1. Click in the page where you want the jump menu to appear. In the Behaviors task pane, click Insert and choose Jump Menu (**Figure 9.41**).

2. When the Jump Menu dialog box appears, click Add (**Figure 9.42**).

3. In the Add Choice dialog box, type a name for this first choice but leave the Value field blank (**Figure 9.43**). (See the first tip.) Click OK.

(continued)

4. When the Jump Menu dialog box reappears, click Add again to continue building the menu list. From here on out, however, click Browse to add URLs for each item in the rest of the list (**Figure 9.44**).

5. Once you finish the menu list, click OK to close the Jump Menu dialog box (**Figure 9.45**).

The menu appears in the page, and Expression Web automatically assigns it an ID name. As you can see in the example, the menu's default width and font size is too big for the layout (**Figure 9.46**). While you could click and drag to reduce the width, that doesn't solve the font size problem (**Figure 9.47**). Fortunately, that ID makes the fix easy.

Figure 9.44 Add URLs for each of your other jump menu choices.

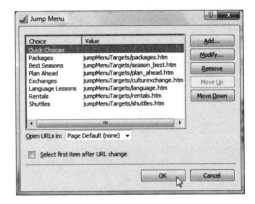

Figure 9.45 Once you finish building the menu list, click OK.

Figure 9.46 The menu appears in the page, and Expression Web automatically assigns it an ID name. The menu's default width and font size, however, need to be adjusted.

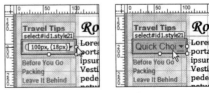

Figure 9.47 You can click and drag to reduce the width (left), but the font size is still too big to fit (right).

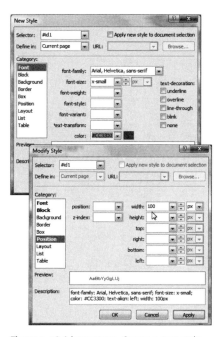

Figure 9.48 A better way: Create a new style using the ID, and then reduce the font (top) and the menu's width (bottom).

Figure 9.49 Fixed: The menu now fits (right) and the new ID-based style appears in the CSS Properties tab (left).

Figure 9.50 The jump menu in action: The first item (Quick Choices) appears without clicking the menu, sparing users the bother if the menu's not relevant to their needs.

6. Click New Style in the Manage Styles tab. When the New Style dialog box appears, type that *exact* ID name in the Selector text box. In the example, the jump menu is named #id1 (top, **Figure 9.48**).

7. Use the dialog box's Font, Block, and Position categories to restyle the menu using a smaller font and narrower width (**Figure 9.48**). Click OK to close the dialog box.

The ID-based style now appears in the CSS Properties tab, and the layout reflects the new styling (**Figure 9.49**).

8. Save your work, and test the menu in a browser (**Figure 9.50**).

(continued)

✔ Tips

- In step 3, the jump menu's first label is what appears in the Web page. By using it to describe the contents—and leaving that line unlinked—you give readers a clue about the menu's purpose without forcing them to click it.

- In step 6, the process of naming and styling IDs is exactly what you did in Chapter 8 when pairing IDs with div tags. For more information, see "To create ID styles for a CSS layout" on page 158. Also, it's true that the number-based names for the jump menu IDs are hard to remember, but leave them be. Unfortunately, if you rename them using the Modify Style dialog box, those IDs disappear—along with your stylings for them.

- In step 7, if you click Apply in the New Style dialog box, the dialog box's name immediately becomes Modify Style. Don't be startled: all your styling information is still right there.

- If you need to change the jump menu's labels, order, or content, double-click its name in the Behaviors task pane.

Adding Media

Adobe Flash videos (.flv files) cannot be inserted directly into an Expression Web 2. Instead, you'll need to use one that's been converted to a SWF (Shockwave Flash) file, a self-running format. You can create SWF files within Flash or similar applications. Or you can buy SWF files on the Web. Expression Web 2's ability to easily insert Windows Media files on pages greatly expands your multimedia choices when creating your Web sites. Windows Media files end with the suffixes .asf, .wm, .wma, .wmv, or .wnd.

Though it's way beyond the reach of this beginner/intermediate book, Expression Web 2 also enables you to install Silverlight-based plug-ins on your pages. Be aware that Silverlight plug-ins cannot be created using Expression Web. Instead, they're built using XAML (Extensible Application Markup Language), typically within Microsoft's Expression Blend program. (For more information on Silverlight, go to: http://www.microsoft.com/silverlight/overview/faq.aspx. (For more on Expression Blend, go to: http://www.microsoft.com/expression/products/overview.aspx?key=blend.)

To insert a Flash .swf file:

1. Using the Design or Code view, click in the page where you want to insert a Flash video (**Figure 9.51**).

2. Do any of the following:

   ◆ Double-click the Flash Movie button in the Media section of the Toolbox task pane (**Figure 9.52**).

   or

   ◆ From the Menu bar, choose Insert > Media > Flash Movie.

3. Use the Select Media File dialog box to navigate to the Flash file you need, which has a .swf suffix (**Figure 9.53**). Select it and click Insert.

   An unstyled placeholder (a container object) for the Flash file appears in the page (**Figure 9.54**).

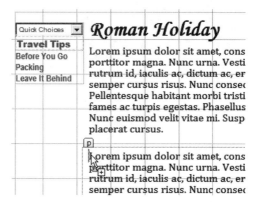

Figure 9.51 Click in the page where you want to insert a Flash or Windows Media file.

Figure 9.52. In the Media section of the Toolbox, double-click the Flash Movie button.

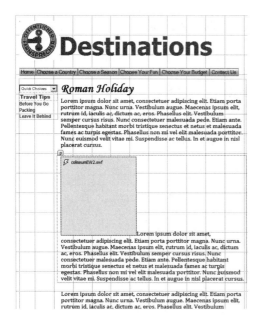

Figure 9.54 After the insert, an unstyled Flash file placeholder appears in the page.

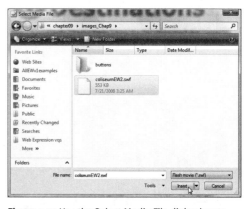

Figure 9.53 Use the Select Media File dialog box to navigate to the Flash file you need, which has a .swf suffix.

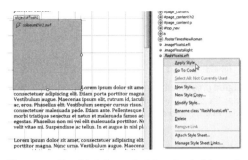

Figure 9.55 To add styling, select the placeholder and then right-click a style in the Manage Styles tab and choose Apply Style.

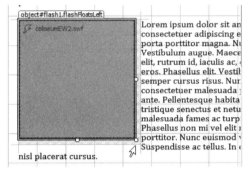

Figure 9.56 With the `.flashFloatsLeft` style applied, the page's text wraps around the movie.

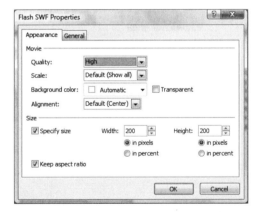

Figure 9.57 Use the dialog box's Appearance tab to set the movie's display quality, scale, background color, alignment, and size.

4. To add styling, select the placeholder. Then right-click a style in the Manage Styles tab and choose Apply Style (**Figure 9.55**). The placeholder's margins reflect the change (**Figure 9.56**). (In the example, `.flashFloatsLeft` is used, which lets the text wrap around the movie placeholder.)

5. If you want to change the movie's properties, double-click the placeholder in the page, or right-click the placeholder and choose Flash SWF Properties in the pop-up menu. When the Flash SWF Properties dialog box appears, you can set the quality, scale, background color, alignment, and size in the **Appearance** tab (**Figure 9.57**). (For more information, see "Setting Flash Properties" on page 185.)

6. To change other properties of the file, click the dialog box's **General** tab, where you can rename the file. More important, use the Playback section to set whether the movie begins on its own (Auto play) and whether it plays once or endlessly (Loop) (**Figure 9.58**). Click OK to close the dialog box and apply your choices.

(continued)

Figure 9.58 Use the dialog box's General tab to set the movie's playback options.

7. Save the page and click Expression Web's Browser Preview button. If you're adding a new file to your Web site, click OK to save it. When your Web browser attempts to display the page, a warning appears atop the page. Right-click it and choose Allow Blocked Content (**Figure 9.59**).

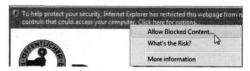

Figure 9.59 When your Web browser attempts to display the page, a warning appears atop the page. Right-click it and choose Allow Blocked Content.

8. A Security Warning dialog box appears. Since it's your own content you're trying to display, click Yes to dismiss the warning (**Figure 9.60**). Your Web browser now shows the movie in the Web page (**Figure 9.61**).

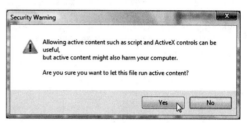

Figure 9.60 A Security Warning dialog box appears. Since it's your own content you're trying to display, click Yes to dismiss the warning.

Figure 9.61 Finally, your Web browser shows the movie in the Web page.

Setting Flash Properties

The Flash SWF Properties dialog box (page 183) has two tabs that control most aspects of how the movie appears in viewers' Web browsers (**Figures 9.57** and **9.58**). The **Appearance** tab choices include:

Quality Use this to set your preferred balance point between a fast-to-download-but-fuzzier rendering of the movie and a slow-to-download-but-sharper version. **Auto Low** favors download speed over quality; **Auto High** favors quality instead of speed.

Scale Your best bet is to choose **Default (Show All)**, which displays the full movie within the frame while keeping the width-height proportions correct.

Background color You'll have a cleaner look if you leave it set to **Automatic** or select **Transparent**. Otherwise, use the drop-down menu to choose one of your document's existing colors.

Alignment Use the drop-down menu to choose how the movie sits within the display area. In most cases, **Default (Center)** is your best bet.

Specify Size Use the Width and Height text boxes to set either in pixels (the movie) or percent (of the page, not the movie's original size). If you do not want the width and height to be the same, first uncheck "Keep aspect ratio."

While the **General** tab includes a number of settings, your choices mostly involve the Playback section:

Name This is not the file's name but its ID, which you can use in a CSS layout as explained on page 158 to 162.

Source URL, Base URL Unless you move the file after it's initially inserted, the Source URL will be filled in, while the Base can remain blank.

Playback These usually are the only settings under the General tab that you change. **Autoplay** lets the movie start without the viewer triggering it manually. **Loop** plays the movie over and over. Selecting **Show menu** allows Web viewers to right-click the movie within their browsers and change some settings in the pop-up menu (**Figure 9.62**). If you select **SWLiveConnect**, the reader's browser starts up Java while loading the Flash player, which can help speed up playback.

CODEBASE If you want, you can paste a URL pointing to the version of Adobe Flash player needed to run the movie, in the unlikely event the viewer doesn't have the necessary version.

Figure 9.62 Selecting Show menu in Figure 9.58 allows Web viewers to right-click the movie and change some settings directly.

To insert a Windows Media file:

1. Using the Design or Code view, click in the page where you want to insert a Windows Media file.

2. Do any of the following:

   ◆ Double-click the Windows Media button in the Media section of the Toolbox task pane.

   or

   ◆ From the Menu bar, choose Insert > Media > Windows Media Player (**Figure 9.63**).

3. Use the Select Media File dialog box to navigate to the Windows Media file you need. Select it and click Insert (**Figure 9.64**). An unstyled placeholder for the Windows Media file appears in the page. (If you want to add styling for the place-holder, select it and right-click a style in the Manage Styles tab and choose Apply Style.)

4. If you want to change the file's behavior, right-click the placeholder and choose ActiveX Control Properties in the pop-up menu. (**Figure 9.65**). (Or just double-click the placeholder.)

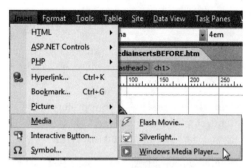

Figure 9.63 To insert a Windows Media file, choose Insert > Media > Windows Media Player.

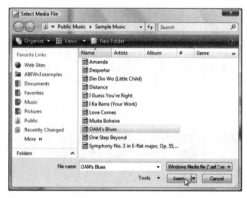

Figure 9.64 Use the Select Media File dialog box to navigate to the Windows Media file you need.

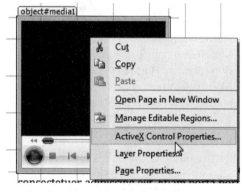

Figure 9.65 To change the file's behavior, right-click the placeholder and choose ActiveX Control Properties. (Or just double-click the placeholder.)

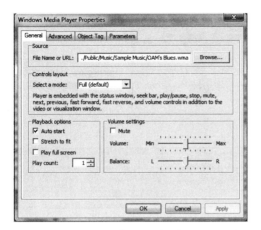

Figure 9.66 Use the Windows Media Player Properties dialog box to change the controls layout, playback options, and volume in the General tab.

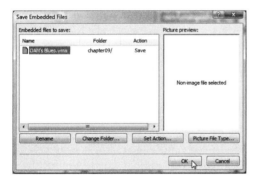

Figure 9.67 Save the page and click OK to save the Windows Media file as part of your Web site.

5. When the Windows Media Player Properties dialog box appears, you can change the controls layout, playback options, and volume in the **General** tab (**Figure 9.66**). The **Advanced** tab offers still more choices for the controls, plus script commands. The **Object Tag** tab lets you change the file's ID, which you can use in a CSS layout as explained on page 158 to 162. The Parameters tab lets you add still more parameters to the file. Click OK to close the dialog box and apply your choices.

6. Save the page and click OK to save the file as part of your Web site (**Figure 9.67**).

7. Click Expression Web's Browser Preview button. When your Web browser starts to display the page, a warning appears atop the page. Right-click it and choose Allow Blocked Content (**Figure 9.59**).

8. Another Security Warning dialog box appears. Since it's your own content you're trying to display, click Yes to dismiss the warning (**Figure 9.60**). Your Web browser now runs the Windows Media file within the Web page.

To insert Silverlight media:

1. Using the Design or Code view, click in the page where you want to insert Silverlight-based media.

2. Do any of the following:

   ◆ Double-click the Silverlight button in the Media section of the Toolbox task pane (**Figure 9.68**).

   or

   ◆ From the Menu bar, choose Insert > Media > Silverlight.

3. In the Insert Silverlight dialog box, click Select Folder (**Figure 9.69**). Use the Select Silverlight Folder dialog box to navigate to the folder containing all the necessary files (there are a bunch). Select it and click Open (**Figure 9.70**).

4. Finally, select the home page for your Silverlight plug-in. The folder of files is imported into your Web site.

✔ Tip

■ Despite whatever hype you may have seen, Silverlight is not intended for use by beginner or intermediate Web page *creators*. Instead, it's aimed at higher-end Web designers/coders using the whole suite of Microsoft's Expression products, especially the interface-design tool Expression Blend. If you started out years ago using Microsoft FrontPage because of its user-friendly features and have upgraded to Expression Web 2, all this may feel like alien territory. If you're interested in learning more, start with the links listed on page 181.

Figure 9.68 To insert Silverlight media, double-click the Silverlight button in the Toolbox.

Figure 9.69 In the Insert Silverlight dialog box, click Select Folder.

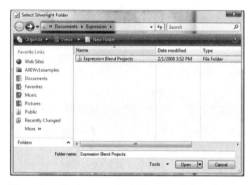

Figure 9.70 Navigate to the folder containing all the necessary files for the Silverlight plug-in.

ADDING TABLES

Expression Web comes with two sets of table tools, one for traditional tables containing columnar data and the other for layout tables containing page elements. This chapter focuses on columnar tables since layout tables are being supplanted by CSS. The shift away from tables for layouts isn't a passing fad. Page-sized tables take longer to load than CSS-based layouts. Plus, tables cannot be easily adjusted to accommodate small displays, such as cell phones. It's true that layout tables let you line up everything on your page just

so. But they completely entangle presentation (how the page looks) with its contents (the information it contains). That guarantees major headaches when you inevitably need to redesign pages and update content.

If you prefer using tables for layouts instead of CSS, see " Using Layout Tables" on page 210. No matter which kind of tables you're creating, you'll find the work goes more quickly using the Tables toolbar (**Figure 10.1**). Turn on the toolbar by choosing View > Toolbars > Tables.

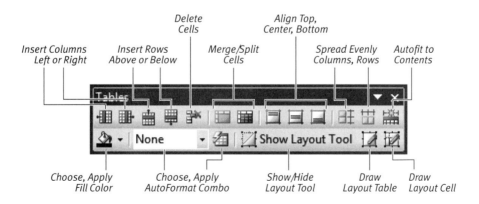

Figure 10.1 Using the Tables toolbar lets you bypass many of menu commands for building tables.

Creating Tables

Tables make it easy to present related text or images in a quick-to-scan form. With their rows and columns composed of individual cells, tables also lend themselves to clean-looking border and color treatments.

To insert a table:

1. Switch to Design view, and click where you want a table placed in the page.

2. Choose Table > Insert Table (**Figure 10.2**).

3. In the Insert Table dialog box (**Figure 10.3**), use the Size section to set how many rows and columns you want for the table.

4. Use the dialog box's Layout section to set the table's alignment, float, and cell padding or spacing.

5. Check Specify width to set the width of the entire table, and use the option buttons to choose whether the width should be absolute (pixels) or relative to the width of the visitor's Web page (percent). Use the same approach for Specify height.

6. Use the Borders area to pick a size for the boundary around the outside of the table. If you like, use the drop-down menu to pick a color and click Browse to add a background picture.

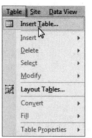

Figure 10.2 To insert a table, choose Table > Insert Table.

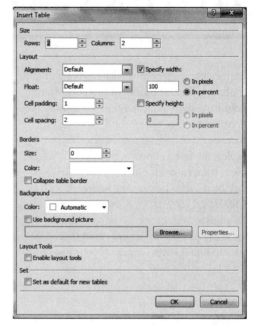

Figure 10.3 Use the Insert Table dialog box to set the table's size and layout.

Figure 10.4 Once you set all the properties for the table, click OK to close the dialog box.

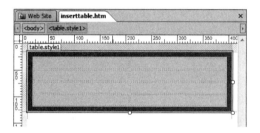

Figure 10.5 The inserted table's width is 100 percent of the page's.

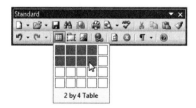

2 by 4 Table

Figure 10.6 For quick tables, click the Insert Table button in the Standard toolbar and drag your cursor to choose how many rows and columns you want.

7. Leave Enable layout tools unselected. (See the first tip about the Set section.) When you're done, click OK (**Figure 10.4**).

A table using those settings appears on the page (**Figure 10.5**).

✔ Tips

■ In the Set section, select Set as default for new tables if that's what you want. To avoid constantly monkeying with the default settings, however, consider inserting a plain table. Then customize the tables when needed as explained in "Formatting Tables and Cells" on page 203.

■ For quick tables using the default settings, click the Insert Table button in the Standard toolbar and drag your cursor into the pop-up table to choose how many rows and columns you want (**Figure 10.6**). Release the cursor, and a table of that size is inserted into the page.

■ If you want a borderless table, set Border size to 0 in the Insert Table dialog box.

■ To proportionately resize the table after it's inserted, press (Shift) and click-and-drag any corner to reduce or enlarge the boundary.

To add table text:

1. Click inside any table cell (**Figure 10.7**).

2. Start typing, and the cell grows to accommodate your text (**Figure 10.8**).

To add table images:

1. Click inside any table cell.

2. Click the Insert Picture from File button in either the Standard or Pictures toolbar (**Figure 10.9**).

3. When the Picture dialog box appears, navigate to the image you want inserted. For details, see "Adding Images" on page 80. Once you find the picture, click Insert.

4. In the Accessibility Properties dialog box, add alternate text for the image, and click OK.

   The image appears in the table cell, which expands to accommodate its size (**Figure 10.10**).

✔ Tip

■ Expression Web includes what it calls AutoFit to automatically fit any material inserted into a cell. First, make sure the Tables toolbar is active, and then after you've inserted an item, click the AutoFit to Contents button (**Figure 10.11**).

Figure 10.7 To add table text, just click inside a table cell.

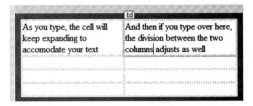

Figure 10.8 As you type, the cell grows to accommodate your text.

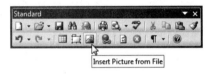

Figure 10.9 To add images to a table, click the Insert Picture from File button.

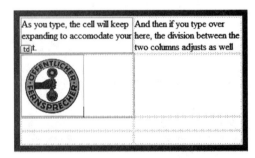

Figure 10.10 When a picture is inserted, the table cell expands to hold it.

Figure 10.11 If material inserted into a cell doesn't fit, click the AutoFit to Contents button in the Tables toolbar.

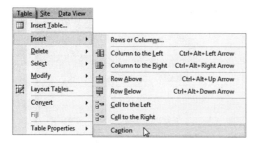

Figure 10.12 To add a caption, click inside the table, and choose Table > Insert > Caption from the menu.

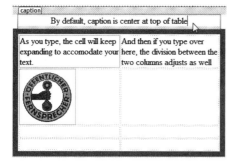

Figure 10.13 By default, captions are centered at the top of tables.

Figure 10.14 Use the Caption Properties dialog box to reposition captions beneath tables.

To add table captions:

1. Click anywhere inside the table, and choose Table > Insert > Caption (**Figure 10.12**).

2. When the cursor appears, it is centered at the top of the table. Type your caption (**Figure 10.13**).

3. Once you've entered the caption, you can change the font or size just like any other text.

✔ Tip

■ You can have the caption appear beneath the table, by right-clicking it and choosing Caption Properties. When the Caption Properties dialog box appears, choose Bottom of table and click OK (**Figure 10.14**). The caption will move to the bottom.

Selecting Table Elements

Unlike many Expression Web procedures, selecting cells, rows, and columns within tables isn't always a click-and-drag affair.

To select a cell:

Do one of the following:

◆ Press (Alt), and click inside any cell. The cell is selected, denoted by its color changing (**Figure 10.15**).

◆ Click anywhere in a cell, and choose Table > Select > Cell (**Figure 10.16**). The cell is selected, denoted by its color changing.

To select multiple cells:

Do one of the following:

◆ To select *adjacent* cells, click and hold your cursor in a cell and then drag the cursor to select additional cells (**Figure 10.17**).

◆ To select *nonadjacent* cells, press (Alt) and click inside any cell, release the cursor, then press (Alt)(Shift), and click another cell. Repeat until you've selected all the cells you need (**Figure 10.18**).

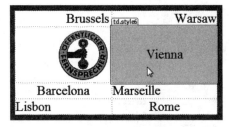

Figure 10.15 To select a cell, press (Alt) and click inside the cell.

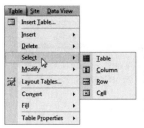

Figure 10.16 To select any element of a table, choose Table > Select and make a choice from the sub-menu.

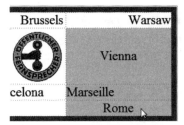

Figure 10.17 To select *adjacent* cells, click the cursor in a cell and then drag the cursor to select additional cells.

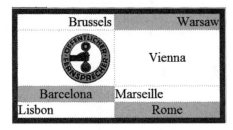

Figure 10.18 To select *nonadjacent* cells, press (Alt) and click inside any cell and then press (Alt)(Shift) as you select other cells.

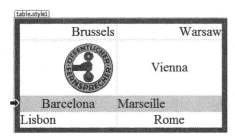

Figure 10.19 To select a row, move the cursor to the left edge until it becomes a black arrow. Click once, and the row is selected.

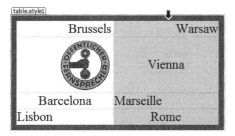

Figure 10.20 To select a column, move the cursor to the top edge until it becomes a black arrow. Click once, and the column is selected.

Figure 10.21 You also can select a table by using the Quick Tag Selector to click the table tag.

To select a row:

Do one of the following:

◆ Click anywhere in a row, and choose Table > Select > Row (**Figure 10.16**). The row is selected.

◆ Click and hold your cursor anywhere in a row, and then drag the cursor to select the rest of the cells in the row.

◆ Move the cursor to the left edge of a row until it becomes an arrow, and then click once. The row is selected (**Figure 10.19**).

To select a column:

Do one of the following:

◆ Click anywhere in a column, and choose Table > Select > Column (**Figure 10.16**). The column is selected.

◆ Click and hold your cursor anywhere in a column, and then drag the cursor to select the rest of the cells in the column.

◆ Move the cursor to the top edge of a column until it becomes an arrow, and then click once. The column is selected (**Figure 10.20**).

To select an entire table:

Do one of the following:

◆ Click anywhere in a table, and choose Table > Select > Table (**Figure 10.16**). The entire table is selected.

◆ Click anywhere in a table, and then use the Quick Tag Selector to click on the table tag (**Figure 10.21**). The entire table is selected.

Changing Table Structure

You can go back and expand a table at any time, whether it's by adding a single cell, a row or column, or even inserting another table into the table.

To add cells:

1. Click in a cell next to where you want to add a cell.

2. Choose Table > Insert > Cell to the Left or Cell to the Right (**Figure 10.22**).

   Depending on your choice, a single cell is inserted into the table just left or right of the selected cell (**Figure 10.23**).

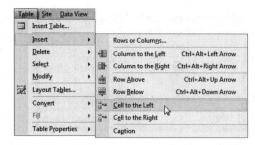

Figure 10.22 To add cells, choose Table > Insert > Cell to the Left or Cell to the Right.

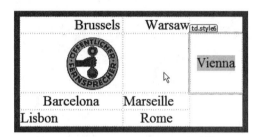

Figure 10.23 A single cell is inserted into the table left of the selected cell.

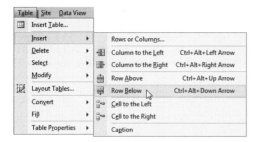

Figure 10.24 To add rows, choose Table > Insert > Row Above or Row Below.

Figure 10.25 If the Tables toolbar is active, you also can add rows by clicking the Row Above or Row Below buttons.

Figure 10.26 A new row is inserted into the table.

Figure 10.27 Use the Insert Rows or Columns dialog box to set the number and placement of the rows you want added.

To add rows:

1. Select a row next to where you want to insert a new row.

2. Choose Table > Insert > Row Above or Row Below (**Figure 10.24**). Or if the Tables toolbar is active, click the Row Above or Row Below buttons (**Figure 10.25**).

The row is inserted into the table (**Figure 10.26**).

✔ Tip

■ You also can insert multiple rows by choosing Table > Insert > Rows or Columns. In the dialog box that appears, select the Rows radio button, set how many rows to insert, and choose whether to insert them above or below the selected row (**Figure 10.27**).

To add columns:

1. Select a column next to where you want to insert a new column.

2. Choose Table > Insert, and then choose Column to the Left or Column to the Right (**Figure 10.28**). Or if the Tables toolbar is active, click the Column to the Left or Column to the Right buttons (**Figure 10.29**).

   The column is inserted into the table (**Figure 10.30**).

✔ Tip

■ You also can insert multiple columns by choosing Table > Insert > Rows or Columns. In the dialog box that appears, select the Columns radio button, set how columns rows to insert, and choose whether to insert them to the left or right of the selected column (**Figure 10.31**).

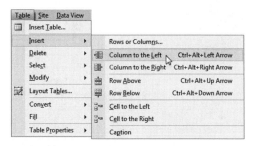

Figure 10.28 To add columns, choose Table > Insert > Column to the Left or Column to the Right.

Figure 10.29 If the Tables toolbar is active, you also can add columns by clicking the Column to the Left or Column to the Right buttons.

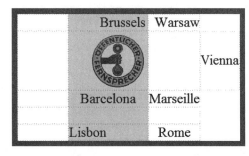

Figure 10.30 A new column is inserted into the table.

Figure 10.31 Use the Insert Rows or Columns dialog box to set the number and placement of the columns you want added.

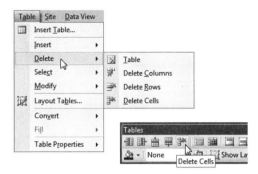

Figure 10.32 To delete part of a table, select it, choose Table > Delete and make a choice in the submenu (left). You also can click the Delete Cells button in the Tables toolbar (right).

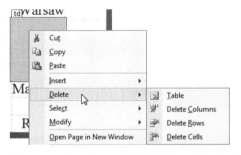

Figure 10.33 You also can right-click the selected part of the table and choose Delete and a submenu.

To delete any part of a table:

1. Select the parts of the table you want to delete, whether it's a cell, a single row, or several rows or columns.

2. Choose Table > Delete Cells, or if the Tables toolbar is active, click the Delete Cells button (**Figure 10.32**). All the selected cells are deleted.

✔ Tip

■ You also can right-click the selected part of the table and choose Delete and a submenu (**Figure 10.33**).

Splitting and Merging Cells

While it's easy to add or delete parts of a table, sometimes you'll want to create or delete an individual cell and not affect the overall dimensions of the rest of the table. That's where the ability to split a cell into two cells, or merge several cells into a single cell, becomes especially handy. You can, for example, create a large cell in the center of a table by merging several adjacent cells and avoid messing up anything else in the table.

To split cells:

1. Click inside the cell you want to split.

2. Choose Table > Split Cells, or if the Tables toolbar is active, click the Split Cells button (**Figure 10.34**).

3. When the Split Cells dialog box appears, choose whether you want the selected cell divided horizontally into rows or vertically into columns (**Figure 10.35**).

4. Use the arrows, or enter numbers directly in the text window, to set the Number of rows or Number of columns you want the cell split into. When you're done, click OK and the cell is split.

✔ Tip

■ You also can right-click the cell and choose Modify > Split Cells from the drop-down menu.

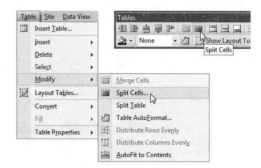

Figure 10.34 To split a cell, click inside it and choose Table > Modify > Split Cells (left), or click the Split Cells button in the Tables toolbar (right).

Figure 10.35 Use the Split Cells dialog box to divide a cell vertically into columns or horizontally into rows.

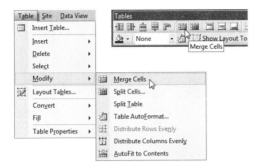

Figure 10.36 To merge cells, select them and choose Table > Modify > Merge Cells (left) or click the button in the Tables toolbar (right).

To merge cells:

1. Select the cells you want merged.

2. Choose Table > Merge Cells, or if the Tables toolbar is active, click the Merge Cells button (**Figure 10.36**). The selected cells are combined into a single cell.

✔ Tip

■ You also can right-click the cell and choose Modify > Merge Cells from the drop-down menu.

Evening Up Rows and Columns

Inevitably as you work on a table, things get messy. Fortunately, there's an easy way to tidy things up by making all your rows the same height or all your columns the same width. The process, by the way, initially seems a bit backward because you select a column to even up the row height and select a row to even up the column width.

To make rows the same height:

1. Select a column containing a cell from each uneven row.

2. Choose Table > Modify > Distribute Rows Evenly (top, **Figure 10.37**). If the Tables toolbar is active, you also can click the Distribute Rows Evenly button (bottom, **Figure 10.37**). The height of the rows is evened up.

To make columns the same width:

1. Select a row containing a cell from each uneven column.

2. Choose Table > Modify > Distribute Columns Evenly (top, **Figure 10.38**). If the Tables toolbar is active, you also can click the Distribute Columns Evenly button (bottom, **Figure 10.38**). The width of the columns is evened up.

Figure 10.37 To make rows the same height, choose Table > Modify > Distribute Rows Evenly (top) or use the button in the Tables toolbar (bottom).

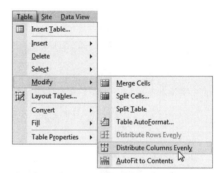

Figure 10.38 To make columns the same width, choose Table > Modify > Distribute Columns Evenly (top), or use the button in the Tables toolbar (bottom).

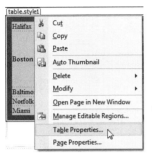

Figure 10.39 To format a table, right-click it and choose Table Properties.

Figure 10.40 Use the Table Properties dialog box to format any aspect of the selected table.

Formatting Tables and Cells

Once you've added a table to your page, put some text and images into it, and perhaps changed its structure, you're ready for the final step: formatting the full table and individual cells. As you reposition or resize a table, Expression Web automatically attaches a class-based style to the table, which you can style directly. By renaming and further modifying this style, you make it easy to reuse later with other tables.

To format tables:

1. Right-click the table, and choose Table Properties (**Figure 10.39**).

2. When the Table Properties dialog box appears (**Figure 10.40**), use the Layout section to set the table's alignment, width, and the cell padding and spacing. The Float drop-down menu lets you float the table to the left or right of text that ordinarily would appear below the table. For more information on floats, see "Using the Float and Clear Tags" on page 150.

3. Use the dialog box's Borders section to set the table's border. For details, see "To format table borders" on the next page.

4. If you want to apply the same color to every cell in the table, use the pop-up box in the Background section to choose your color.

5. Once you're done, click OK, and the changes are applied to your table.

To format table borders:

1. Select the table to which you want borders applied, and then right-click and choose Table Properties (**Figure 10.39**).

2. When the Table Properties dialog box appears, use the Borders section to set the Size (width) of your border (**Figure 10.41**). Use the Color pop-up box to pick a color.

3. Once you set the width and color, click OK or click Apply (right), and the border changes are applied (left) (**Figure 10.42**).

✔ Tip

■ Use the Table AutoFormat icon in the Tables toolbar to preview and modify a variety of preformatted table settings (**Figure 10.43**). Once you learn the names of the preformatted choices, you can reach them directly by clicking the drop-down menu next to the Table AutoFormat button (**Figure 10.44**).

Figure 10.41 Use the Borders section the Table Properties dialog box to set the size (width) and color of your border.

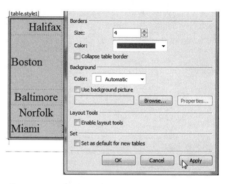

Figure 10.42 Once you set the width and color, click OK or click Apply (right) and the border changes are applied (left).

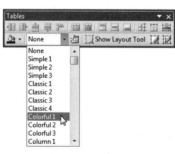

Figure 10.44 Click the drop-down menu in the Tables toolbar to quickly reach Table AutoFormats.

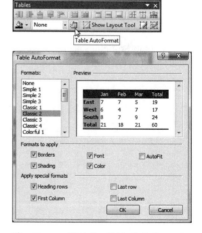

Figure 10.43 Click the Table AutoFormat button in the Tables toolbar to preview the preformatted table choices.

Figure 10.45 To see the style properties attached to a table, roll the cursor the style name in the CSS Properties tab (or Manage Styles tab).

Figure 10.46 In the Manage Styles tab, right-click the style and choose Rename class in the drop-down menu.

Figure 10.47 Give the class a new name that indicates its purpose, such as .mainTablestyle.

Figure 10.48 Right-click the renamed style, and choose Modify Style.

To format tables using CSS:

1. Any repositioned or resized table automatically has a class-based style attached to it. To see its properties, roll your cursor over the style name in the Manage Styles tab or the CSS Properties tab. In the example, it's .style1 (**Figure 10.45**).

2. In the Manage Styles tab, right-click the style, and choose Rename class in the drop-down menu (**Figure 10.46**).

3. In the Rename Class dialog box, give the class a new name that indicates its purpose, such as .mainTablestyle in the example (**Figure 10.47**). Click OK to close the dialog box.

4. In the Manage Styles tab (or CSS Properties tab), right-click the renamed style and choose Modify Style (**Figure 10.48**).

    Use the categories in the Modify Styles dialog box to make other changes to the table's style (**Figure 10.49**). When you're done, click OK to close the dialog box. For more information on modifying styles, see Chapter 7 on page 123.

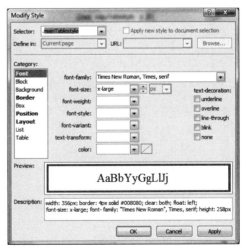

Figure 10.49 Use the categories in the Modify Styles dialog box to make other changes to the table's style.

FORMATTING WITH CSS

To format cells:

1. Select the cell or cells you want to format, and then right-click and choose Cell Properties (**Figure 10.50**).

2. When the Cell Properties dialog box appears (**Figure 10.51**), use the Layout section to change the alignment and size of the selected cell.

3. Check Specify width and Specify height if you want to set the cell's dimensions. Choose pixels to make either dimension absolute or percent to make it relative to the size of the viewer's Web browser window.

4. If you want to have the selected cell span more than one row or column, enter a number in the Rows spanned window or Columns spanned window.

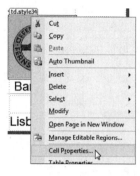

Figure 10.50 To format selected cells, right-click and choose Cell Properties.

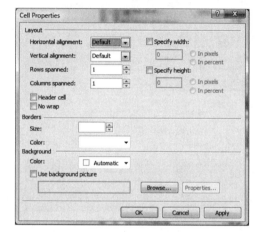

Figure 10.51 Use the Cell Properties dialog box to change the cell's alignment, size, and borders.

Figure 10.52 Once you've made your changes, click OK to close the dialog box and apply the changes to the cell.

Figure 10.53 The cell with the new formatting applied.

5. Use the Borders section to set the thickness and color of the cell's border and the Background section for the color within the cell. When you're done making changes, click OK (**Figure 10.52**)

The dialog box closes, and the changes are applied to the selected cell(s) (**Figure 10.53**).

✔ Tips

- In the Layout section, check Header cell if you want the selected cells to act as labels for rows or columns within a table. Expression Web makes the text in header cells boldfaced. The No wrap option keeps the selected cell's text all on one line.

- While the Cell Properties dialog box offers the option of setting border colors for individual cells, it's more effective visually to adjust borders for an entire table. For details, see "To format table borders" on page 204.

- You may find it faster to use the Tables toolbar to change a cell's alignment or color.

Adding Excel Spreadsheets

There are two ways to display Excel spreadsheet data in your Web pages. The first, as explained below, simply creates a table based on the Excel data *at the time you import it.* In other words, it's static data—not a "live" spreadsheet that's dynamically updated. The second method serves up live data that changes based on users' input. Unfortunately, it only works if your Web site's host service uses Active Server Pages (ASP) and Microsoft's Internet Information Services (IIS). Because of that limitation, we don't cover serving dynamic pages. But it couldn't be simpler to present static Excel data.

To add static Excel data:

1. Use Excel to select and save as a new document only the portion of the spreadsheet you need. Open the new document and choose File > Save As.

2. In the Save As dialog box, set the Save as type drop-down menu to CSV (Comma delimited) before clicking Save (**Figure 10.54**).

3. Excel warns you that some formatting *may* be lost but that's the cost of converting to CSV, so click Yes (**Figure 10.55**). Your document reappears in the CVS format, though it probably won't look much different than before.

4. Select the content you need and copy it ([Ctrl][C] or right-click and choose Copy) (**Figure 10.56**).

Figure 10.54 Set the Save as type drop-down menu to CSV (Comma delimited) before clicking Save.

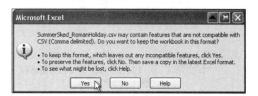

Figure 10.55 When Excel warns you that some formatting *may* be lost, click Yes.

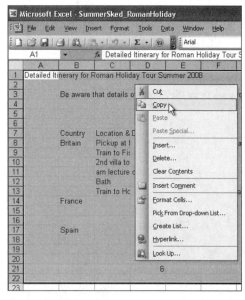

Figure 10.56 Select the content you need and copy it.

Figure 10.57 In Expression Web, use the Standard toolbar's Insert Table button to create a single-cell table.

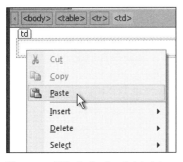

Figure 10.58 Paste the Excel data into the Expression Web single-cell table.

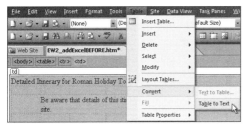

Figure 10.59 Select the entire table and choose Table > Convert > Table to Text.

5. Back in Expression Web in Design view, click in the page where you want the data to appear. Use the Standard toolbar's Insert Table button to create a single-cell table (**Figure 10.57**).

6. Paste the Excel data copied in step 4 into the new single-cell table ([Ctrl][V] or right-click and choose Paste) (**Figure 10.58**). The table expands to hold the Excel data.

7. Select the entire table and choose Table > Convert > Table to Text (**Figure 10.59**). The table is converted to text. Now you can use Expression Web's HTML and CSS tools to further format the text as needed.

✔ Tip

■ In step 5, you also can paste the data into the table in Code view. Just remember that you'll need to refresh your view ([F5]) before the data will appear in the Design view.

ADDING EXCEL SPREADSHEETS

Using Layout Tables

If you're old school and simply do not want to switch to using CSS positioning for your layouts, layout tables offer the most control for the greatest number of Web browsers. Be sure to turn on the Tables toolbar (View > Toolbars > Tables) (**Figure 10.60**). The Layout Tables task pane includes twelve prebuilt page-sized layout tables to speed your work (Task Panes > Layout Tables). You also have the option of directly drawing a layout table.

To add a prebuilt layout table:

1. Switch to Design view, open a blank page, and click the prebuilt layout you want to use in the Layout Tables task pane (**Figure 10.61**).

   The layout table is inserted into the page with size labels marking each cell (**Figure 10.62**).

2. To resize any cell, click the size label at its side or top (**Figure 10.63**).

Figure 10.60 Before working with layout tables, turn on the Tables toolbar (View > Toolbars > Tables).

Figure 10.61 Click the prebuilt layout you want to use in the Layout Tables task pane.

Figure 10.62 The layout table is inserted into the page with size labels marking each cell.

Figure 10.63 To resize any cell, click the size label at its side or top and make a choose in the drop-down menu.

Figure 10.64 Use the Row Properties or Column Properties dialog boxes to set a precise pixel size.

Figure 10.65 The size label changes to reflect your pixel entry.

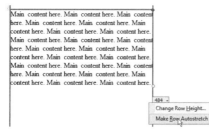

Figure 10.66 Choose Make Row (or Column) Autostretch to have the cell automatically shrink or grow as its content changes.

Figure 10.67 With Autostretch applied, the cell's height shrinks to fit the content.

3. In the drop-down menu, choose Change Row Height (or Change Column Width) if you want to pick an exact value. Use the dialog box to enter a new value (in pixels), and click OK (**Figure 10.64**).

The row or column changes size (**Figure 10.65**).

or

In the drop-down menu, choose Make Row (or Column) Autostretch to have the cell automatically shrink or grow as its content changes (**Figure 10.66**).

The row or column changes size (**Figure 10.67**).

4. Add your content to the layout (**Figure 10.68**).

✔ Tips

- If at any point, the size handles disappear, just click the Show Layout Tool button in the Layout Tables task pane or the Tables toolbar.

- You can resize the rows and columns at any time.

Figure 10.68 Once you finish sizing the layout, you can begin adding images, text, and headers.

To draw a layout table:

1. Click on the page where you want to add the table, and then click the Draw Table button in the Tables toolbar or Tables task pane.

2. A pencil icon appears on the page. Click and drag the pencil until the dashed box is roughly the size of the table you want, and release the cursor button (**Figure 10.69**).

   A layout table appears on the page with a dimension label attached to each side. (**Figure 10.70**).

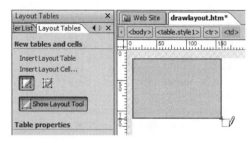

Figure 10.69 Draw a layout table by activating the Show Layout Tool button (left) and dragging the pencil icon across the page (right).

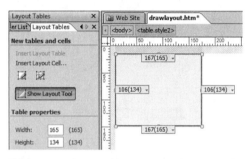

Figure 10.70 A layout table appears on the page with a dimension label attached to each side.

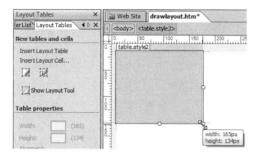

Figure 10.71 Deactivate the Show Layout Tool button (left), and then click and drag any corner to resize the layout table (right).

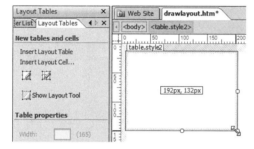

Figure 10.72 Once you release the cursor, the layout table assumes its new size.

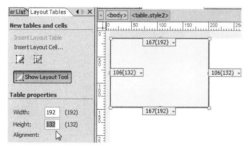

Figure 10.73 If you need more precision in resizing the layout table, use the width or height boxes in the Layout Tables task pane.

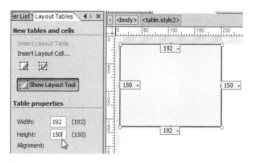

Figure 10.74 Press [←Enter] and the layout table change to its new size.

3. To resize the table, deactivate the Show Layout Tool button by clicking it so that the labels disappear from the table. Click and drag any corner to resize the table (**Figure 10.71**).

The table assumes its new size (**Figure 10.72**). If you want to add cells to the layout table, see "To draw layout cells" on the next page. Otherwise, add content to your table.

✔ Tip

■ In step 3 if you need more precision, enter a new width or height in the text boxes in the Layout Tables task pane and press [←Enter] (**Figure 10.73**). The table changes size (**Figure 10.74**).

To draw layout cells:

1. Click to select the table in which you want to add a cell. Click the Show Layout Tool button to display the table's dimension labels, and then click the Draw Layout Cell button (**Figure 10.75**).

2. Move the cursor into the table where it becomes a pencil icon (**Figure 10.76**).

3. To draw a single cell, click and drag the pencil until the dashed box is roughly the size you want, and release the cursor button.

   A cell appears in the table (**Figure 10.77**).

   or

   To draw multiple cells, one after the other, press and hold down Ctrl while you draw each cell. Release the cursor button once you draw the last cell.

   The multiple cells appear in the table (**Figure 10.78**).

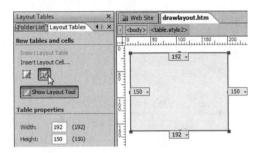

Figure 10.75 To further divide the layout table into columns and rows, activate the Show Layout Tool and click the Draw Layout Cell button.

Figure 10.76 Move the cursor into the table where it becomes a pencil icon.

Figure 10.77 To draw a single cell, click and drag the pencil until the dashed box is roughly the size you want and release the cursor button.

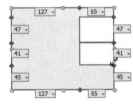

Figure 10.78 To draw multiple cells, one after the other, press and hold down Ctrl while you draw each cell.

DRAWING LAYOUT CELLS

Figure 10.79 To resize a cell, right-click it and choose Cell Properties from the drop-down menu.

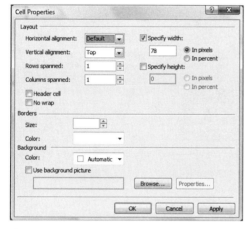

Figure 10.80 Use the Cell Properties dialog box to precisely resize a cell.

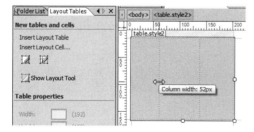

Figure 10.81 You also can resize a cell by turning off the Show Layout Tool button (left) and then clicking-and-dragging the cursor to change the column width or row height (right).

4. To resize a cell, right-click it and choose Cell Properties from the drop-down menu (**Figure 10.79**). Use the Cell Properties dialog box to precisely resize the cell plus change any other cell properties as desired (**Figure 10.80**). Click OK to close the dialog box and apply the changes.

   or

   Deactivate the Show Layout Tool button by clicking it so that the labels disappear from the table. Move your cursor over the row or column containing the cell. When the cursor becomes a two-headed arrow, click and drag the row or column to resize it (**Figure 10.81**). Release the cursor to apply the change.

5. Add your content to the layout.

ADDING FORMS

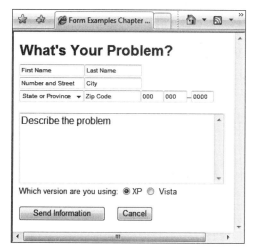

Figure 11.1 Forms enable you to collect a variety of information from your users.

Forms enable you to collect information from your users by presenting them with questions, option buttons, check boxes, and multiple-choice menus (**Figure 11.1**). You begin by creating a form. All the fields you need to collect information are inserted inside that form. The last step involves setting how the form results are saved on the server hosting your Web site. For creating forms, you'll use the Form Controls section within the Toolbox task pane (**Figure 11.2**). Open it by choosing Task Panes > Toolbox and then expanding the Form Controls section.

Toolbox	✕
⊟ **HTML**	
⊞ **Tags**	
⊟ **Form Controls**	

Advanced Bu...   Drop-Down Box   Form
Group Box   Input (Button)   Input (Check...
Input (File)   Input (Hidden)   Input (Image)
Input (Passw...   Input (Radio)   Input (Reset)
Input (Submit)   Input (Text)   **A** Label
Text Area

Figure 11.2 The Form Controls section of the Toolbox task pane contains all you need for creating forms.

Creating Forms

Creating the form itself is always your first step, since it acts as the "container" for holding all the fields into which users enter information.

To create a form:

1. Open an existing Web page, or create a new page, and make sure you're in Design view. Click in the page where you want the form inserted, and double-click the Form button in the Toolbox task pane (**Figure 11.3**).

   The form, bounded by a dashed outline, is inserted into the page (**Figure 11.4**).

2. Since all your fields must go inside the form, click-and-drag the boundary to give yourself plenty of working room (**Figure 11.5**). You're now ready to add whatever form fields you need. For details, see "Adding Form Fields" on the next page.

Figure 11.3 To create a form, double-click the Form button in the Toolbox task pane.

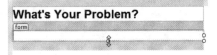

Figure 11.4 The form, bounded by a dashed outline, is inserted into the page.

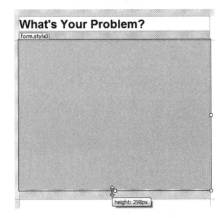

Figure 11.5 To give yourself some working space, click and drag any handle on the form's side or corner.

Form Validators

A popular feature in FrontPage, built-in form validation, is not available in Expression Web. If your site host uses Microsoft's Internet Information Services (IIS), you can use Expression Web's ASP.NET controls, which include validators. You'll find them at the bottom of the Toolbox task pane.

Figure 11.6 Create some text to identify the field for the user, and then click where you want to add the accompanying text box.

Figure 11.7 Double-click the Input (Text) button in the Toolbox task pane.

Figure 11.8 When the one-line field appears in the page, right-click it and choose Form Field Properties.

Figure 11.9 Use the Text Box Properties dialog box to give your field a name, initial value, size, and password.

Adding Form Fields

Expression Web includes more than a dozen form fields to give you lots of flexibility in gathering information from your site's visitors. Of all the form fields (sometimes called form controls), the text box is probably the one you'll use the most. While only the most commonly used fields are explained here, the process for adding the other buttons works similarly.

To add a text box:

1. Click in the form where you want to add the field, typically next to text you've entered to identify the field for users (**Figure 11.6**).

2. Double-click the Input (Text) button in the Toolbox task pane (**Figure 11.7**).

3. When the one-line field appears in the page, right-click it and choose Form Field Properties from the drop-down menu (Alt Enter) (**Figure 11.8**).

4. In the Text Box Properties dialog box, Expression Web assigns the field an arbitrary name, such as Text1 (top, **Figure 11.9**). You don't need to change it, since it's invisible to site visitors and used by form-handling scripts. If you do change it, make sure the new name has no spaces and uses standard ASCI characters (bottom, **Figure 11.9**).

(continued)

ADDING FORM FIELDS

5. If you want text to appear inside the one-line box, such as "Enter your name here," type it in the Initial value text box. (See the first tip below.)

6. If you want, set how many characters wide the line should be, and enter a number for the field's tab order within the form. (See the second tip.)

7. If the field will be used for a password, choose Yes; otherwise, leave it set to the default No.

8. When you're done, click OK.

   The properties are applied to the one-line text field (**Figure 11.10**).

✔ Tips

◆ In step 5, if you enter an Initial Value, you can skip also adding a text label next to the field. It's also cleaner looking than Expression Web's Label form button (**Figure 11.11**). The button is meant to help voice browsers figure out when text is serving as a label for an adjacent field, but the feature still has some kinks to work out.

◆ If you need to resize a text box, don't bother using the Text Box Properties dialog box. Just click the box and use one of corner or side handles to enlarge or shrink it.

Figure 11.10 When you're done, the properties are applied to the one-line text field.

Figure 11.11 The awkward Label form button still has some kinks to work out.

ADDING FORM FIELDS

Figure 11.12 To add a text area, double-click the Text Area button in the Toolbox task pane.

Figure 11.13 If you want text to appear inside the box, type it in the Initial value text box.

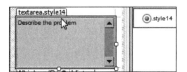

Figure 11.14 A class-based style tag automatically is applied to a text area when you resize it.

Figure 11.15 By renaming the style, you can apply it to other text areas for a more uniform look.

Adding a Text Area

While a text box contains only a single line of text, a text area can be as large as you need.

To add a text area:

1. Click in the form where you want to add the text area.

2. Double-click the Text Area button in the Toolbox task pane (**Figure 11.12**).

3. When the field appears in the page, resize it as needed by click-and-dragging any side or corner handle.

4. Right-click the field, and choose Form Field Properties ($\boxed{\text{Alt}}\boxed{\text{Enter}}$).

5. Expression Web assigns the field an arbitrary name in the dialog box. If you change it, use a name with no spaces and only ASCII characters so scripts can read it.

6. If you want text to appear inside the box, such as "Enter your name here," type it in the Initial value text box (**Figure 11.13**).

7. If you aren't happy with your initial sizing, set the character width and line number using the text boxes. Enter a number for the field's tab order within the form.

8. When you're done, click OK.

   The properties are applied to the text area (**Figure 11.14**).

✔ Tips

- Whenever you resize a text area, a class-based style tag is applied (**Figure 11.14**). You can attach that style to an external style sheet and apply elsewhere to create similar text areas (**Figure 11.15**).

- In step 5, the Password field option just hides the input with *s to keep others from seeing it. It's not encrypted or more secure than the rest of your site.

ADDING A TEXT AREA

Adding Group Boxes

Group boxes offer a way to gather a bunch of buttons and labels into a single tidy box. This can be especially handy for multiple check boxes and option buttons, since you can easily move them while preserving their relative positions.

Figure 11.16 To add a group box, double-click the Group Box button in the Toolbox task pane.

To add a group box:

1. Click in the form where you want to add the group box.

2. Double-click the Group Box button in the Toolbox task pane (**Figure 11.16**).

3. When the group box appears in the page, resize it as needed by click-and-dragging any side or corner handle.

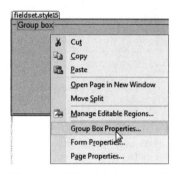

Figure 11.17 Right-click the box, and choose Group Box Properties from the drop-down menu.

4. Right-click the box, and choose Group Box Properties from the drop-down menu (**Figure 11.17**).

5. In the Group Box Properties dialog box, the box is labeled Group box (top, **Figure 11.18**). Unlike the field box names, this name *will* be seen by users and isn't used by scripts, so give it a name that lets your visitors know its purpose. Choose an alignment, and click OK (bottom, **Figure 11.18**).

   The properties are applied to the group box (**Figure 11.19**).

Figure 11.18 A group box's label will be visible, so give it a name that lets your visitors know its purpose.

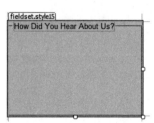

Figure 11.19 Now labeled, the group box is ready to help organize your other fields.

Figure 11.20 To add a check box, double-click the Input (Checkbox) button in the Toolbox task pane.

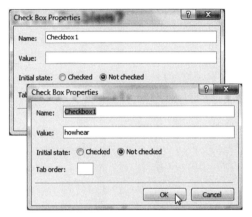

Figure 11.21 The content of the Value field, which is not seen by the user, cannot be left blank.

Adding Check Boxes and Radio Buttons

Unlike text boxes in which users can enter a variety of information, check boxes and option buttons have only two states: on (checked) or off (not checked). The main difference between check boxes and radio (option) buttons is that users can choose *several* check boxes, while radio buttons force users to make *one* choice among several.

To add a check box:

1. Click in the Group Box form where you want to add the check box.

2. Double-click the Input (Checkbox) button in the Toolbox task pane (**Figure 11.20**).

3. When the check box appears in the page, right-click it and choose Form Field Properties from the drop-down menu ((Alt)(Enter)).

4. In the Check Box Properties dialog box, the field is assigned an arbitrary name, such as Checkbox1 (top, **Figure 11.21**). If you change it, make sure the new name has no spaces and uses standard ASCI characters so it can be used in scripts.

5. The content of the Value field, which is not seen by the user, cannot be left blank. Type any word that helps you quickly identify the response field (bottom, **Figure 11.21**).

(continued)

6. By default, the check box's Initial state is Not checked. Choose Checked if you're sure most users will want the box already selected.

7. Enter a number for the field's tab order within the form, and click OK.

The properties are applied to the check box.

8. Because the check box is quite small, be sure to label it. If you need more check boxes, repeat the steps.

9. Once you're done, take a look at the check boxes in a Web browser and decide if any need adjustment (**Figure 11.22**).

Figure 11.22 As seen in a browser, the group box helps organize multiple check boxes.

Figure 11.23 To add radio buttons, double-click the Input (Radio) button in the Toolbox task pane.

Figure 11.24 In the Option Button Properties dialog box, the field is assigned an arbitrary Group name. Value cannot be left blank.

Figure 11.25 Once you're done, take a look at the radio buttons in a Web browser.

To add radio (option) buttons

1. Click in the Group Box form where you want to add the option button, typically next to text asking users to choose among several option buttons.

2. Double-click the Input (Radio) button in the Toolbox task pane (**Figure 11.23**).

3. When the radio button appears in the page, right-click it and choose Form Field Properties from the drop-down menu ((Alt)(Enter)).

4. In the dialog box, the field is assigned an arbitrary name, such as Radio1 (**Figure 11.24**). If you change it, make sure the new name has no spaces and uses standard ASCI characters so it can be used in scripts.

5. The content of the Value field, which is not seen by the user, cannot be left blank. Type any word that helps you quickly identify the response field .

6. By default, the button's Initial state is Not selected. Choose Selected if you're sure most users will want the button already selected.

7. Enter a number for the field's tab order within the form, and click OK.

   The properties are applied to the radio button.

8. Because the radio button is so small, type a label next to it. If you need more check boxes, repeat the steps.

9. Once you're done, take a look at the radio buttons in a Web browser, and decide if any need adjustment (**Figure 11.25**).

ADDING RADIO BUTTONS

Adding Submit and Reset Buttons

After filling in a form's various fields, users need a way to send that information to your server. That's the job of the submit button. The reset button, its natural opposite, cancels those field submissions so users can start over. Both are examples of push buttons, sometimes called command buttons, because they exist strictly to trigger an action.

Figure 11.26 To add a submit button, double-click the Input (Submit) button in the Toolbox task pane.

To add a submit button:

1. Click in the form where you want to add the submit button, typically at the bottom of the form so that visitors don't click it until after they've finished filling in your form.

2. Double-click the Input (Submit) button in the Toolbox task pane (**Figure 11.26**).

3. When the button appears in the page, right-click it, and choose Form Field Properties from the drop-down menu.

4. In the Push Button Properties dialog box, the field is assigned an arbitrary name, such as Submit1 (top, **Figure 11.27**). If you change it, make sure the new name has no spaces and uses standard ASCI characters so it can be used in scripts.

5. Like the group box label, the push button value/label *will* be seen by users, so give it a name that clues visitors in about what to do. (Submit, the default, might make perfect sense to us computer types, but regular folks may find Send clearer.) (bottom, **Figure 11.27**).

6. Leave the button type set to Submit, add a number for the field's tab order in the form, and click OK.

   The button appears in the form (**Figure 11.28**).

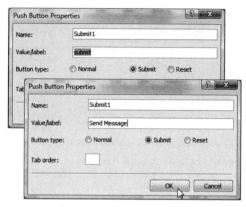

Figure 11.27 Submit, the default, makes sense to computer types, but regular folks may find Send clearer.

Figure 11.28 The submit button typically appears at the bottom of the form.

Figure 11.29 To add a reset button, double-click the Input (Reset) button in the Toolbox task pane.

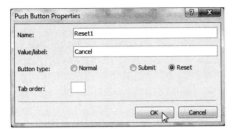

Figure 11.30 Just like the submit button, the Value/label *will* be visible, so give it a name that tells visitors what to do.

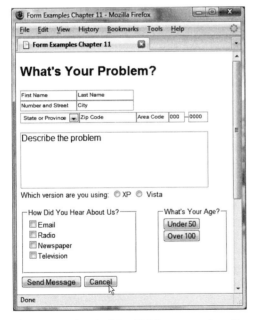

Figure 11.31 Take a look in a Web browser, and see if anything needs adjustment.

To add a reset button:

1. Click in the form where you want to add the reset, usually right next to the submit button at the bottom of the form.

2. Double-click the Input (Reset) button in the Toolbox task pane (**Figure 11.29**).

3. When the button appears in the page, right-click it, and choose Form Field Properties from the drop-down menu.

4. In the Push Button Properties dialog box, the field is assigned an arbitrary name, such as Reset1 (**Figure 11.30**). If you change it, make sure the new name has no spaces and uses standard ASCI characters so it can be used in scripts.

5. Just like the submit button, the value/label *will* be seen by users, so give it a name that clues visitors in about what to do.

6. Leave the button type set to Reset, add a number for the field's tab order in the form, and click OK.

   The button appears in the form. Take a look in a Web browser, and see if anything needs adjustment (**Figure 11.31**).

Saving Form Results

To save all the data submitted from your forms, you need to choose which form handler to use. If you've been running FrontPage and your Web site host still uses the FrontPage server extensions, you don't have to change a thing. They should continue saving results to your choice of a file, an email, or a database. If you're starting fresh with Expression Web, however, or want to use a nonproprietary setup, you can save the results using a variety of widely available custom scripts (API, CGI, and ASP). If that's alphabet soup to you, contact your Web site's host to see what's best for your needs.

To save results if not using FrontPage extensions:

1. In Design view, right-click your form and choose Form Properties from the drop-down menu (**Figure 11.32**).

2. In the Form Properties dialog box, choose Send to other and use the default Custom ISAPI, NSAPI, CGI, or ASP Script (**Figure 11.33**).

3. Use the Form properties section if you want to give the form another name or if you want to set a target frame for the form.

4. Click Options to reach the Options for Custom Form Handler dialog box (**Figure 11.34**).

5. In the Action text box, type the URL where you've stored your script. Leave Method set to post and the Encoding type text box blank.

6. Click OK to close the Options dialog box. Click OK to close the Form Properties dialog box as well.

    The settings are applied to the form.

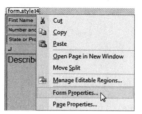

Figure 11.32 To control how form results are saved, right-click the form and choose Form Properties.

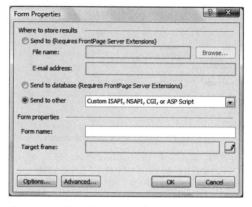

Figure 11.33 If you're *not* using FrontPage extensions, choose Send to other and use the default Custom ISAPI, NSAPI, CGI, or ASP Script.

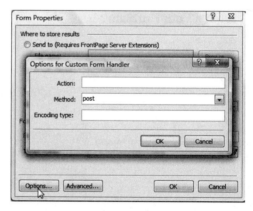

Figure 11.34 Click Options to reach the Options for Custom Form Handler dialog box.

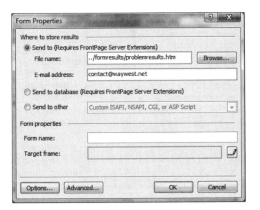

Figure 11.35 Use the Form Properties dialog box to choose whether form results are saved as a file, email, database record, or customized data.

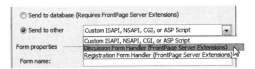

Figure 11.36 If using FrontPage extensions, you can use the drop-down menu to select a form handler.

Figure 11.37 The File Results tab lets you set the file's name, format, and other details of saving the data.

Figure 11.38 The File format drop-down menu offers nine choices for formatting the results data.

To save results if using FrontPage extensions:

1. In Design view, right-click the form and choose Form Properties from the drop-down menu.

2. In the Form Properties dialog box (**Figure 11.35**), choose:
   - ▲ Send to, and then use Browse to select a destination file on your *server* or enter an email address. If you like, you can save the results as a file *and* as email. (For details see "FrontPage Extension Options" below.)
   - ▲ Send to database. Click the Options button to set up the details of the database. (For details see "FrontPage Extension Options" below.)
   - ▲ Send to other, and use the drop-down menu to select a form handler (**Figure 11.36**) (For details see "FrontPage Extension Options" below.)

3. Use the Form properties section if you want to rename the form or if you want to set a target frame for the form.

4. Assuming you've already set your options, click OK to close the dialog box.
   The settings are applied to the form.

FrontPage Extension Options

The Options button in the Form Properties dialog box triggers different choices based on what you do step 2 of "To save results if using FrontPage extensions" above.

Send to File name: In the dialog box that appears, click the File Results tab (**Figure 11.37**). Pick a file format using the drop-down menu (**Figure 11.38**). Check Include field names if you want to pair the values of each form field with its name. Unless you choose HTML, Latest results at end is checked. To create a second results file, perhaps in another format, use the Optional second file section to enter a new name or browse to an existing file. Click OK to return to the Form Properties dialog box.

Send to E-mail address: In the dialog box that appears, click the E-mail Results tab (**Figure 11.39**). Use the E-mail format drop-down menu to choose a text format. Check Include field names if you want to pair the values of each form field with its name. By default, the email's subject line would be Form Results, though you can type another choice. In the Reply-to line text box, enter an address for the sender of the email. Click OK to return to the Form Properties dialog box.

Send to database: In the dialog box that appears, click the Database Results tab to configure your database connection (**Figure 11.40**). Click OK to return to the Form Properties dialog box.

Send to other: One of two dialog boxes appears, depending on your choice in the Send to other drop-down menu (**Figure 11.41**). Configure as needed, and when you're done, click OK to return to the Form Properties dialog box.

Figure 11.39
The E-mail Results tab lets you set the message's address, format, subject line, and reply address.

Figure 11.40
The Database Results tab lets you port the form results to an existing or new database.

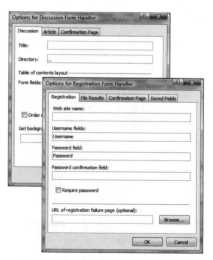

Figure 11.41 The Discussion and Registration form handlers can be precisely configured for your needs.

PUBLISHING THE SITE

12

Two crucial steps remain before you actually copy your local files to a Web server. First, use Expression Web to check if any pages have problems, such as broken hyperlinks or slow-to-download files. Second, look at every page with a Web browser to check its general appearance. When you're ready to publish, you'll need to have an Internet Service Provider (ISP) lined up to host your site, unless you are copying the files to an inhouse intranet.

Checking Your Site

Expression Web's reporting tools make it much easier and faster to get your site ready to publish. Instead of depending on your Web browser to find every problem, Expression Web provides a site summary of possible problems. The reports feature also makes it easy to mark any pages on the site that you do not want published yet, avoiding the all-too-common problem of accidentally publishing pages prematurely.

To check and fix your site:

1. Choose Site > Reports > Site Summary, or click the Web Site tab and use the drop-down menu just below it to select Site Summary (**Figure 12.1**).

   When the Site Summary appears in the main window, it lists general site information and any problems (**Figure 12.2**).

2. If the summary lists problems, such as broken hyperlinks, double-click that line in the report to see a list of the problem pages.

3. To fix an individual page in the list, double-click it and the appropriate dialog box appears, allowing you to fix the problem (**Figure 12.3**).

4. Repeat steps 2 and 3 until you've fixed all the problems.

Figure 12.1 To check for problems, choose Site > Reports > Site Summary (left) or, if the Reports view is visible, click the drop-down menu below the Web Site tab and choose Site Summary (right).

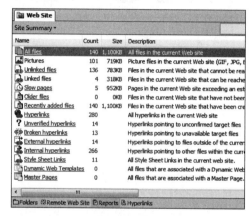

Figure 12.2 The Site Summary report provides a detailed overview of your site's problems. Double-click any line for details.

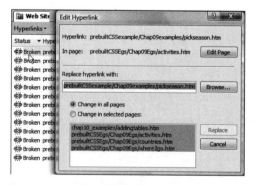

Figure 12.3 Double-click a listing in the Broken Hyperlinks report (left), and the Edit Hyperlink dialog box appears (right), enabling you to fix the link.

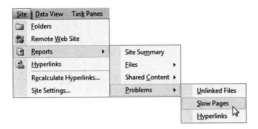

Figure 12.4 To examine a particular problem, choose Site > Reports > Problems and make a choice in the submenu.

Figure 12.5 To see hidden folders, check Show hidden files and folders under the Advanced tab.

Figure 12.6 To change the publish status of pages, right-click the selected file(s) and check or uncheck Don't Publish.

Figure 12.7
Files marked with a small red X will *not* be published.

✔ Tips

■ You can switch to Reports view any time by clicking the Reports button at the bottom of the main window (**Figure 12.2**).

■ To return to the Site Summary after you've double-clicked to select an individual problem report, click the Web Site tab and use the drop-down menu just below it to select Site Summary.

■ If you want to check for a particular problem, such as slow pages, choose Site > Reports > Problems and make a choice in the submenu (**Figure 12.4**).

■ By default, any files placed inside hidden folders (those preceded by an underscore) will not appear in the Site Summary or problem reports. To have those files show up in reports, choose Site > Site Setting, click the Advanced tab, and check Show hidden files and folders (**Figure 12.5**).

To change the publish status of pages:

1. Choose Site > Reports > Files > All Files, or click the Web Site tab and use the drop-down menu just below it to select Files > All Files.

   When the file list appears in the main window, select the files whose publish status you want to change. (Use ⟮Shift⟯-click to select adjacent files, ⟮Ctrl⟯-click for nonadjacent files.)

2. Right-click the selected file(s) and in the drop-down menu check Don't Publish (**Figure 12.6**). The selected files are marked with a small red X, showing that they will *not* be published (**Figure 12.7**).

   or

   To publish files marked with red Xs, right-click them and in the drop-down menu uncheck Don't Publish. The red Xs are removed and the files *will* be published the next time you upload your site.

Publishing to the Web

After you've fixed your Web pages and marked which ones should be published, you should preview them in several Web browsers. Once you've fixed any problems found in the browsers, you're finally ready to copy your Web site files from your local hard drive to the Web server you'll be using. Before you start, you'll need to know the server address that you'll be copying your files to, plus a user name and password to gain access to the server. Check with the Web server's administrator if you need help.

By the way, the publishing process includes an option to create a backup of your local site. In fact, making a backup site should be the first thing you do before actually publishing to the remote Web server. The steps are nearly the same, so consider it a practice run. Given how easy it can be to accidentally overwrite your local Web site files with the remote Web site's files, making a backup site first is always a smart move.

To set the publish destination and options:

1. Open the Web site you want to publish, and choose Site > Remote Web Site, or click the Remote Web Site button at the bottom of the main window (**Figure 12.8**).

2. Within the Web Site window, click the Remote Web Site Properties button (**Figure 12.9**).

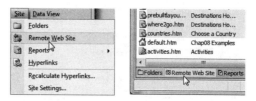

Figure 12.8 To start the publishing process, choose Site > Remote Web Site (left) or click the Remote Web Site button at the bottom of the main window (right).

Figure 12.9 To add or change a publishing destination, click the Remote Web Site Properties button.

Figure 12.10 In the Remote Web Site Properties dialog box, choose the server type that matches your Web server setup.

Figure 12.11 Use the Optimize HTML tab to remove various coding items from your Web pages before they are published.

3. In the Remote Web Site Properties dialog box (**Figure 12.10**), do one of the following:

▲ Choose FrontPage Server Extensions if your remote Web server includes the extensions. If you're converting an existing FrontPage site to Expression Web, this will be your first choice.

▲ Choose WebDAV if your remote Web server uses this common file checkout system.

▲ Choose FTP if you are running a plain vanilla Web server and want to move files to it using the long-standing File Transfer Protocol. This is the choice Expression Web selects by default since it's likely to be the main choice for everyone except those sticking with FrontPage extensions.

▲ Choose File System if you want to make a backup copy of your local Web site before actually publishing it. The backup copy can reside on your own computer or another computer anywhere on the Internet.

4. Once you make your choice, type a URL or local file path in the Remote Web site location text window or click Browse to navigate to a folder on the Web or an internal server. Unless you want to change the default settings in the other two tabs, Optimize HTML or Publishing, skip to step 7.

5. Click the dialog box's Optimize HTML tab, and if you like, select the first checkbox, When publishing, optimize HTML by removing the following elements (**Figure 12.11**). Then select any of the other checkboxes to remove various coding items from your Web pages before they are published. (See the tip.)

(continued)

6. Click the dialog box's Publishing tab, and if you like, change the defaults for whether all or just changed local pages are published to the remote site (**Figure 12.12**). Use the Changes section to set how Expression Web determines which pages have changed.

7. Once you've made your choices, click OK to close the dialog box.

The Remote Web Site view reappears with the files for the local Web site on the left and the empty remote Web site on the right (**Figure 12.13**). To publish the site, see the next page.

✔ Tip

■ In step 5, you have the choice of optimizing the coding in your Web site by removing unnecessary HTML to help the pages download more quickly (**Figure 12.11**). Examples would be any white space you've left in to make the code easier to read or explanation comments you've added for yourself or others creating the site. Expression Web can strip out this code for the remote site while preserving it in your local site.

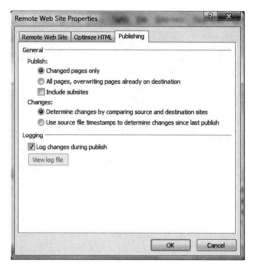

Figure 12.12 Use the Publishing tab to choose whether all or just changed local pages are published to the remote site.

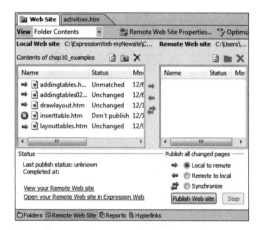

Figure 12.13 Before publishing, the Remote Web Site view lists the local site files on the left and the empty remote Web site on the right.

Figure 12.14 To publish your site, in the lower right of the main window, select Local to remote and click Publish Web site.

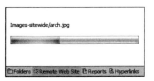

Figure 12.15 Expression Web compiles a list of the files that need to be uploaded to the server.

Figure 12.16 When the Connect to dialog box appears, enter the user name and password assigned to you by the ISP or the server's administrator.

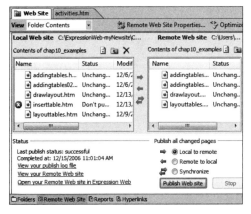

Figure 12.17 After publishing, the Remote Web Site view lets you compare what's on the local and remote Web sites.

To publish your site:

1. At the bottom of the Web site window, click the Remote Web Site button. In the lower right of the main window, select Local to remote and click Publish Web site (**Figure 12.14**).

2. There is a brief pause as Expression Web compiles a list of the files that need to be uploaded to the Web server (**Figure 12.15**).

3. When the Connect to dialog box appears, type the user name and password that your ISP or Web server administrator assigned you (**Figure 12.16**).

4. After another pause (the time depends on how many new pages you're uploading and your connection speed), Expression Web begins copying your Web pages to the Web server. Depending on your site setup, a series of dialog boxes may appear. Either click Ignore and Continue to resume the publishing process or Cancel to double-check your settings.

   When the upload finishes and the Web site window reappears, the files from the local site (on the left) have been copied to the Web site (on the right) (**Figure 12.17**).

5. Using the choices in the window's lower left, you can see a log of the files, see the now-published site in your Web browser, or see your remote site from within Expression Web. Take a look at the site to make sure everything looks right. If you spot problems, fix the local version of the page and upload it again. If everything looks good, you're done.

(continued)

✔ Tips

- Depending on how your Internet connection's configured, you may need to connect to your Web server before clicking the Publish Web site button in the Remote Web Site view.

- After the first time you publish your Web site, and assuming your remote Web site settings remain the same, you can save yourself some steps whenever you need to update the Web server files. Just choose File > Publish Site (**Figure 12.18**), or click the Publish Web site button in the Remote Web Site view. The site is published without opening any dialog boxes. If you need to change any publishing settings, click the Remote Web Site Properties button in the Remote Web Site view.

- You can use the publishing process to download files from the remote site to your local site (**Figure 12.14**). You also can select Synchronize, which puts the most current version of each file on both sites.

- If you choose to overwrite pages already on the Web site, Expression Web alerts you if that will change the site's navigation structure. You'll have the choice of leaving the structure as is, replacing it with your changes, or merging both versions by using only the newest pages.

Figure 12.18 Once you publish a site, you can publish further changes just by choosing File > Publish Site.

INDEX